MASTERING EMOTIONAL INTELLIGENCE FOR TEENS

THRIVE IN THE DIGITAL AGE WITH A POSITIVE
MINDSET, BUILD RESILIENCE, EMBRACE
GROWTH, AND NAVIGATE SOCIAL MEDIA

ALLIE SIMON

CONTENTS

INTRODUCTION
EMBARKING ON THE VOYAGE OF EMOTIONAL INTELLIGENCE

"The greatest discovery of any generation is that a human can alter his life by altering his attitude." – William James

---

HEY, have you ever felt like you're on an emotional rollercoaster that just won't stop? One minute, you're cracking up over a hilarious meme, and the next, you're disappointed that your post didn't get as many likes or views as you had hoped. It's like navigating through a maze without a guide. Then, you throw in the endless game of comparing yourself to everyone else, especially on social media, while also trying to figure out who you are, and things start to pile up.

That's where emotional intelligence steps in, being a bright, guiding star, helping you through the maze that is your life. Emotional intelligence involves recognizing, understanding, and managing your emotions while also understanding how others feel. Think of it as a toolkit that can help you handle stress, make decisions more effectively, build stronger relationships, and navigate the complexities of teenage life. Seriously, I cannot stress the importance of emotional intelligence, especially today, when you are faced with challenges that didn't even exist when your parents were your age.

So, I wrote this book with a purpose: to give you that toolkit. It's packed with practical tips to help you handle your emotions, recover from setbacks, empathize with others, and uncover your true self. It's not just about getting by; it's about flourishing in every part of your life, whether you're online or offline.

You'll face these modern challenges directly because this book is set up to walk you through the important parts of emotional intelligence one step at a time. Get ready for relatable stories, enjoyable exercises, quizzes to learn more about yourself, and thought-provoking questions. Each section is crafted to take you on a personal journey.

As you flip through these pages, stay open-hearted and curious because you're embarking on a journey that will transform how you navigate life's twists and turns, making you more resilient, empathetic, and, you guessed it, emotionally intelligent.

So, are you ready to begin? Let's plunge into this adventure with all the excitement and curiosity you can summon, ready to unlock the mysteries of emotional intelligence. Here we go!

CHARTING THE INNER SEAS: UNDERSTANDING EMOTIONS

"Emotions are not problems to be solved. They are signals to be interpreted." – Vironika Tugaleva

YOUR LIFE MAY OFTEN FEEL like it's moving rather quickly, with your emotions fluctuating unpredictably, influenced by everything from the weather to a comment on social media. But what if you could actually get to know these feelings better, figure out where they come from, and even predict what might set them off? This chapter invites you into the fascinating world of emotions, where science and everyday experiences mix together, giving you tips that could help you handle your emotional ups and downs.

The Science of Emotions: What Happens Inside Us?

Your brain is the control center for your emotions. Inside its intricate design, the amygdala and prefrontal cortex are the main parts that influence how you feel every day.

Understanding the Brain

The amygdala acts like a vigilant guard, always scanning your surroundings for anything important and ready to react to threats or rewards. This small, almond-shaped part of your brain triggers quick, gut-level reactions that have helped humans survive. In contrast, the prefrontal cortex, which handles decision-making, takes a more thoughtful approach. It considers the amygdala's reactions against what it knows from past experiences, current goals, and future consequences, often acting as a moderator.

For example, when you get a text from a friend inviting you out, the amygdala might spark excitement, but the prefrontal cortex will remind you of your busy week ahead. This balance between instant emotional reactions and careful thinking shapes a lot of how you feel.

Emotional Responses

Your body reflects the emotional battle going on in your brain through physical reactions. Think about when you're scared: your heart races, your palms get sweaty, and you start breathing faster. These responses are controlled by the autonomic nervous system, which gets your body ready to face danger or run away—the famous "fight or flight" response. "Freeze" and "Fawn" have also been added as possible responses. Sometimes, your body is unable to move (freeze). On the other hand, if the danger is, for example, a person, your body might have you try to please the other person to avoid the conflict (fawn). The rush of adrenaline that accompanies fear is part of your body's way of ensuring you're ready to act swiftly in the face of potential threats.

Neuroplasticity and Emotions

One of the best things about your emotional brain is its ability to change, known as neuroplasticity. Every new experience, thought, and feeling can rewire your brain's pathways, allowing you to develop healthier emotional habits over time. For example, practicing mindfulness can strengthen the connections between your prefrontal cortex and amygdala, helping you stay calm and composed in stressful situations.

This plasticity means that your emotional patterns aren't fixed. By actively creating positive emotional experiences and using emotional regulation techniques, you can shape your brain to become more resilient and adaptable.

The Role of Hormones

Various hormones flowing through your body deeply affect your emotions. Cortisol, known as the "stress hormone," can make you more alert and ready to tackle challenges. However, if your cortisol levels stay high for too long, it can lead to burnout and exhaustion. I've had issues with my cortisol levels before—they were outside the normal range and didn't follow the standard pattern. Cortisol should be highest in the morning and decrease throughout the day, but mine was lowest in the morning and highest at night. This mismatch affected my productivity and emotions during the day.

On the other hand, serotonin, often called the "feel-good hormone," helps stabilize your mood and promotes happiness. Activities like exercise, sunlight exposure, and certain foods can boost serotonin levels, providing easy ways to improve your mood. For example, I often do a little "happy dance" when I eat something delicious.

Understanding how your brain and body work together to shape your emotions shows that your feelings aren't random. They're influenced by a complex mix of neural signals and hormones. Knowing this helps you manage your emotions with more awareness and control.

Why Emotional Intelligence Matters More Than IQ

Academic scores and intellectual achievements often get all of the attention during your teenage years. However, emotional intelligence

(EQ) plays a crucial role in shaping your success, happiness, and relationships. Unlike IQ, which measures cognitive skills, EQ focuses on your ability to understand, control, and express your emotions, as well as manage your relationships wisely and empathetically.

Success Beyond Academics

The idea that good grades are the key to success is being challenged by evidence showing that emotional intelligence (EQ) might be more important. Studies consistently show that people with high EQ tend to have more satisfying careers, stable and fulfilling relationships, and better mental health. This doesn't mean that IQ and academic skills aren't important, but managing emotions, handling social situations, and making smart decisions are crucial for well-rounded success. For example, in the workplace, technical skills are important, but so are teamwork, stress management, and effective communication.

Emotional Intelligence in Leadership

In leadership, the importance of EQ is even clearer. Leaders with high emotional intelligence can inspire, motivate, and connect with their team members on a deeper level, creating an environment of trust and productivity. They are skilled at recognizing their own emotions and those of others, using this emotional insight to guide their thinking and behavior, and managing emotions to adapt to different situations or achieve goals. This contrasts with the stereotypical image of leaders who rely solely on intellectual skills or authority. Emotionally intelligent leaders value empathy, active listening, and constructive feedback, fostering a workplace culture that promotes growth, learning, and collaboration. I had a manager, Laine, who was the epitome of an emotionally intelligent leader at one of my jobs as a speech-language pathologist. She was extremely knowledgeable but also humble, compassionate, generous, and kind. Her feedback was always presented as a learning opportunity, and she never disregarded or belittled her coworkers.

Resilience Factor

Another key aspect of emotional intelligence is resilience, the ability to bounce back from setbacks and challenges. People with high EQ have a toolkit of coping strategies that help them navigate life's ups and downs smoothly. They manage their emotions during stress, seek support when needed, and see challenges as opportunities for growth. This resilience is vital for personal well-being and staying on track toward goals, no matter what obstacles come up. Instead of being thrown off by setbacks, those with high emotional intelligence can assess the situation, adjust their strategies, and keep moving forward.

Empathy in a Connected World

Empathy—being able to understand and share someone else's feelings —has never been more crucial in our interconnected world. With just a tap on a screen, you can connect with people worldwide, exposing yourself to diverse perspectives, experiences, and challenges. People with high EQ thrive in this global setting because they can easily see things from others' perspectives, fostering understanding and connection across cultural and geographical boundaries. This empathy not only strengthens personal relationships but also helps navigate the complexities of the digital age, from managing online interactions to tackling global issues with compassion.

As you explore the many roles of emotional intelligence in your life, it's clear that EQ isn't just a nice-to-have skill—it's fundamental to how you interact with the world and yourself. Whether it's finding success in your career and relationships or leading with compassion and resilience, emotional intelligence has a profound and widespread impact. By nurturing your EQ, you open doors to a more fulfilling, connected, and resilient life, ready to tackle the challenges of the modern world with confidence and empathy.

Recognizing Your Emotions: The First Step to Emotional
Intelligence

Recognizing and labeling your emotions is like checking the forecast
within yourself. Just as you grab an umbrella when it's cloudy outside,
understanding your internal emotional weather helps you navigate
life more effectively. This section dives into the process of identifying
emotions, why labeling them is important, exercises to boost
emotional awareness, and the delicate interplay between your
thoughts, emotions, and actions.

Identifying Emotions

Learning to accurately identify emotions is like having a map when
you're in unfamiliar territory. It starts with tuning into the subtle
signals your body sends you. The flutter of anxiety feels different
from the warmth of joy; recognizing these sensations is the first step.
Mindfulness plays a crucial role here. It means paying close attention
to the present moment and observing thoughts and feelings without
judgment.

For example, when you feel frustrated because of a canceled plan,
take a moment to pause. Notice how your body reacts. Do you feel
tension in your shoulders? Heaviness in your chest? These physical
sensations are clues to the emotions you're experiencing. Your body
often communicates with you without using words.

The Power of Labeling

Once you figure out what you're feeling, putting a name to it is super
powerful. Studies have found that naming your emotions can actually
make them feel less intense and easier to deal with. It's like giving
your brain a tool to understand what's going on, which helps to calm
things down.

For example, if you say to yourself, "I'm bummed that the plans got
canceled," it can change how you see the situation. Instead of feeling

totally overwhelmed, you can see it as something you can handle. It doesn't make the feeling go away, but it gives you more control over it, rather than it controlling you.

Emotional Awareness Exercises

Consistent practice is the secret sauce to getting better at understanding your emotions. Check out these exercises meant to help you get more in tune with how you're feeling:

- **Mindful check-in:** Take a few moments throughout your day to stop and see how you're doing. Close your eyes, take some deep breaths, and ask yourself, "What am I feeling right now?" Then, name the emotions you recognize.
- **Emotion tracking:** Keep a journal where you jot down important moments in your day and how you felt during them. As you keep track, you'll notice trends in how you react to different things over time.
- **The five whys:** When you're hit with a big emotion, keep asking yourself "why" you feel that way. Then, ask "why" four more times for each answer you come up with. This trick can help you uncover the deeper reasons behind your feelings that you might not have realized before.
- **Body scan meditation:** Try this meditation where you mentally go through your body, from your head down to your toes, noticing any feelings without judging them. It's a great way to link up physical sensations with how you're feeling emotionally, which can make it easier to figure out what's going on inside you.

At the end of this book, you'll discover a special 21-Day EQ Challenge tailored just for you.

The Link Between Thoughts and Emotions

Your thoughts and feelings are like best friends who talk all the time, influencing each other non-stop. Knowing this connection is super important for handling your emotions well. Negative thoughts can kick off a chain reaction of emotions, which can then lead to even more negative thoughts, creating a tough cycle to break. But the good news is, you can flip the script by changing your thoughts.

For instance, if you keep telling yourself, "I'll never get the hang of this," you might start feeling down and frustrated. But if you catch onto this pattern, you can challenge those negative thoughts and swap them for something more positive, like, "I'm getting better every day." That switch can spark feelings of hope and motivation instead.

This whole connection between thoughts and emotions also shines a light on how we talk to ourselves. The way we speak inside our heads can either lift us up or drag us down. Building a supportive inner voice can really boost how you feel emotionally.

This whole dance of recognizing emotions, giving them names, doing awareness exercises, and understanding how thoughts and feelings lay the groundwork for building emotional intelligence. As you get better at navigating your inner emotional world, you're basically arming yourself with tools to tackle life's ups and downs with more strength and understanding.

Emotional Intelligence: Your Superpower in a Digital World

In the colorful mosaic of today's teenage experience, the online world shines bright, buzzing with activity and energy. It's a place where borders fade away, friendships stretch across the globe, and chats carry on into the wee hours. But amidst this digital wonderland lie some challenges. As a teen in this era, you're weaving through a land-scape where the divide between online and offline emotions blurs more each day, empathy can seem scarce, and staying true to yourself is a constant test of courage.

Navigating Emotions in the Digital World

The digital age throws some unique emotional hurdles our way. Despite its perks, social media can sometimes feel like walking a tightrope, balancing the joy of connection with the fear of comparison and self-doubt. Every like, comment, and share has the power to lift you up or bring you down, making it super important to manage your digital emotions well.

One trick that works is setting limits on how much time you spend on social media. Maybe you decide not to check it right when you wake up or before you go to bed, times when you might be more sensitive. It also helps to pick what you see on your feed carefully. Instead of stuff that makes you compare yourself to others or feel down, fill your feed with things that make you happy and inspired. I did this on Instagram by unfollowing everyone and starting fresh. I filled my feed with puppies, cool artists, funny stuff, and things that motivated me. You can do the same thing on any social media platform, including TikTok.

Another smart move is mindfulness. Just like you'd stay present and non-judgmental in meditation, try bringing that attitude to your social media time. Before you react to something you see online, take a moment to breathe and think. This little pause can totally change how you feel and respond to stuff online.

Empathy in the Digital Realm

Empathy, which is all about understanding and sharing someone else's feelings, is just as important online as it is offline. When we're communicating through screens, picking up on emotional cues can be a bit trickier, but it's still super crucial.

One way to boost your online empathy skills is through active listening, or in this case, active reading. Pay close attention not just to what's being said, but how it's being said. Look out for emotional hints in the words and tone. When you respond, try to match that emotional vibe to show that you get where the other person is coming from.

Another handy trick is to ask open-ended questions. This encourages the other person to share more and shows that you're genuinely interested in what they have to say. It's a simple but effective way to build empathy and have deeper connections, even when you're chatting online.

Building Digital Resilience

Alongside the perks of the digital world come its downsides, like exposure to negativity and cyberbullying (which we will discuss in more depth in Chapter 6). That's where digital resilience comes in—it's all about being able to handle and bounce back from online challenges to keep your emotional well-being intact.

A big part of this resilience is realizing that you're in control of your online space. Use privacy settings and reporting tools to shield yourself from harmful interactions. And remember, it's totally fine to block or unfollow anyone or anything that brings you down.

Another important aspect is reaching out for support. Talk to friends, family, or mentors about what you're going through online. They can give you fresh perspectives and advice, and sharing your struggles reminds you that you're not alone in this digital maze.

Lastly, work on building up your self-worth from within. Affirmations can be a great tool for this. Remind yourself of your strengths and values to help buffer against the negative effects of online criticism or cyberbullying.

. . .

Authentic Self-Expression in the Digital World

In a space where everyone's showing off their best sides and perfect moments, it can feel like you have to fit into that mold, too. But being true to yourself online is super important for your emotional well-being. It helps you form real connections and pushes back against the pressure to be perfect all the time.

To express yourself authentically online, start by thinking about what really matters to you. Share stuff that lines up with your interests, values, and beliefs. It not only feels better, but it also brings together a community of people who vibe with you.

But remember, being authentic doesn't mean you have to spill everything. It's about staying true to who you are in what you choose to share. It's totally fine to keep some stuff private. The key is making sure the version of yourself you show online matches who you are in real life.

And hey, brace yourself for some mixed reactions. Not everyone will dig what you have to say, and that's okay. What matters most is that you're being real. Over time, this honesty leads to deeper connections and a sense of fulfillment.

During your teen years, emotional intelligence isn't just a skill – it's like having superpowers. It helps you navigate the online world gracefully, stand strong against the tough stuff, understand others even through screens, and be your true self in a world of filtered images. Just so you know, these abilities aren't just handy online; they make every part of your life richer, giving you a solid foundation of emotional intelligence that supports you both online and off.

The Four Pillars of Emotional Intelligence

Think of emotional intelligence as a sturdy tree, rooted deep and reaching high, able to weather life's storms. Its power comes from four main pillars: Self-Awareness, Self-Management, Social Awareness, and Relationship Management. Each pillar is important on its own, but they also work together, like branches intertwining, to help you grow emotionally and form strong connections with others.

Self-Awareness

At the core of emotional intelligence is self-awareness – being able to recognize and understand your own emotions. It's all about tuning in to those little shifts inside you and knowing how they affect what you think and do.

For example, you're in a situation and suddenly you feel annoyed. Self-awareness kicks in, and you stop to ask yourself, "What's really bothering me?" Maybe you realize you're not actually mad at the person in front of you but are stressed about a big test coming up. This kind of insight is gold. It stops you from taking out your stress on the wrong person and helps you deal with what's really bugging you.

Developing self-awareness includes:

- **Checking in with yourself regularly:** Pause several times a day to figure out how you're feeling and why you might be feeling that way.
- **Reflecting on emotional reactions:** After big emotional moments, take some time to think about what caused those feelings and how you reacted to them.
- **Seeking feedback:** Don't hesitate to ask others for their thoughts on your emotional patterns. Sometimes, they can offer insights that you might not notice on your own.

Self-Management

Self-management means being able to handle and control your emotions, especially when things get tough. It's about making decisions about how you respond to your feelings, rather than just letting them take over.

For example, let's say you're feeling nervous about a presentation. Self-management techniques like taking deep breaths or imagining things going well can help you calm down and stay focused. It's also about not reacting right away when you're upset. Instead of lashing out when you're angry, you might choose to take a break, go for a walk, and deal with the situation more calmly later on.

Key strategies for self-management include:

- **Identifying coping mechanisms that work for you:** This could be physical exercise, journaling, or talking things out with a friend.
- **Practicing relaxation techniques:** Mindfulness, meditation, and controlled breathing exercises can help soothe emotional turbulence.
- **Setting goals to improve your emotional control:** Push yourself to work on the areas where managing your emotions is tough, and celebrate your progress along the way.

Social Awareness

This pillar is all about understanding what others are feeling. It's about picking up on the little signs that show how someone else is doing and being able to imagine how they might be feeling. Empathy is super important for getting through social stuff smoothly and building stronger bonds with people.

Think about a friend who's acting more low-key than usual. Social awareness helps you spot this shift and maybe prompts you to check in with them. They might open up about a family problem they're dealing with. Understanding this, you can give them the support they need, whether it's a shoulder to lean on or just giving them some space.

To boost your social awareness, try these tips:

- **Tune in to nonverbal cues:** Keep an eye on body language, tone of voice, and facial expressions – they often reveal more about how someone's feeling than what they're saying.
- **Be an active listener:** When someone's talking, give them your full attention without thinking about what you'll say next.
- **Reflect on what you've heard to make sure you get it:** Repeat back what they've said to show you understand, and try to see things from their point of view.
- **Show empathy:** Make an effort to understand where the other person is coming from and respond in a way that shows you get how they're feeling.

Relationship Management

Being able to handle interactions and build strong connections is the peak of emotional intelligence. It brings together self-awareness, self-management, and social awareness to navigate the twists and turns of human relationships.

Effective relationship management means knowing when to give a little and when to stand your ground, how to talk about your feelings in a helpful way, and how to sort out disagreements without damaging your bond. It's about building trust through consistency, understanding, and respect in how you deal with others.

For instance, let's say you and a friend hit a rough patch. Instead of letting anger take over, you use what you know about your feelings and theirs to talk things out calmly and find a solution together. You listen to each other, share your thoughts without pointing fingers, and work as a team to fix things.

Tips for building solid relationships include:

- **Practicing clear and compassionate communication:** Be honest and kind when you express your thoughts and feelings. Make sure to listen carefully to the other person and validate their perspective.
- **Learning conflict resolution skills:** See conflicts as chances to make your bond stronger by working through problems and getting to know each other better.
- **Showing appreciation and gratitude:** Take the time to tell the important people in your life how much you appreciate them. Let them know they matter to you.

Navigating your teenage years can often feel like exploring uncharted territory. But armed with the four pillars of emotional intelligence as your guide, you can navigate the emotional ups and downs of adolescence with confidence and purpose. Whether it's understanding your own emotions, handling them well, forming strong connections with others, or fostering healthy relationships, these pillars provide a solid foundation for personal development and harmonious social interactions. As you work on honing these skills, you'll discover that you're not just getting by – you're thriving, even in the face of life's challenges and chances.

2

NAVIGATING THROUGH STORMS: BREATHING YOUR WAY TO CALM

"The body benefits from movement, and the mind benefits from stillness." – Sakyong Mipham

PICTURE yourself with a remote control in your hand. This remote isn't for your TV, it's for your stress and anxiety levels, like turning down the volume on a song. But guess what? You've got something even more amazing than any gadget out there. It's called breathing. Yep, every time you breathe in and out, you've got the power to change how you feel and think, and how you deal with everything around you. In this chapter, we're going to talk about breathing techniques. They're simple, but they're like magic for bringing calm into your life, especially when being a teenager gets crazy.

The Science of Breathing: A Gateway to Calm

Understanding how you breathe goes beyond just staying alive; it's a connection between your body and mind. It has a direct impact on how you feel emotionally and how stressed you are. When you're stressed, your breathing gets shallow and fast, which is your body's way of gearing up to fight or run away. But this kind of breathing can keep you feeling tense, both physically and mentally. The good news is, you can change this pattern. By practicing controlled breathing exercises, you can trigger your body's relaxation response. This means your heart rate slows down, your blood pressure drops, and you start feeling more peaceful. With the right breathing techniques, you can dial down the stress, helping you concentrate better, make decisions, and just enjoy the moment.

Deep Breathing Exercises: Step-by-Step Stress Relief

Here's a step-by-step guide to deep breathing exercises that can help you hit the reset button on your stress levels:

1. **Find your zen zone:** Pick a quiet spot where you can chill out without any interruptions. It could be your room, a cozy corner in the library, or even a peaceful park bench.
2. **Get comfy:** Sit or lie down in a position that feels good for you. If you're sitting, make sure to keep your back nice and straight.
3. **Hand placement:** Put one hand on your belly and the other on your chest.
4. **Inhale slow and steady:** Take a slow breath in through your nose. Feel your belly rise as it pushes your hand out. Try to keep your chest still.
5. **Hold it:** Hold your breath for a moment, or a quick pause.
6. **Exhale nice and easy:** Now, breathe out slowly through your mouth or nose, whichever feels more natural. Feel your belly fall as you let the air out.
7. **Repeat and relax:** Keep up this breathing rhythm for a few minutes. Pay attention to how your belly rises and falls

with each breath. Let yourself unwind and destress as you go along.

Adding just a few minutes of deep breathing to your daily routine can make a big difference in lowering stress and bringing a sense of calm.

Rhythmic Breathing: Finding Your Emotional Rhythm

Now, let's talk about rhythmic breathing, which takes things up a notch by adding a specific pattern to your breaths that can really boost your emotional balance. Here's a technique called "4-7-8 breathing":

1. **Inhale smoothly for 4 seconds:** Take a quiet breath in through your nose, counting to 4 slowly.
2. **Hold for 7 seconds:** Hold your breath for a steady count of 7 seconds.
3. **Exhale strongly for 8 seconds:** Breathe out forcefully through your mouth, making a "whoosh" sound, for a count of 8 seconds.
4. **Repeat:** Do this cycle for four breaths, keeping the rhythm going.

Give it a try whenever you need to find your emotional groove.

You can use this method anytime, anywhere, but it's especially handy right before something stressful, like a big test or giving a presentation. It can help you switch gears from feeling anxious to feeling calm and ready to tackle whatever comes your way.

Breathing Apps and Tools: Your Digital Breathing Coach

In a world where our smartphones feel like an extra limb, it's only natural to turn to technology for a little wellness boost. Luckily, there are plenty of apps out there ready to be your digital breathing coach, reminding you to take a breather when you need it most. Here are a few you might want to check out:

- **Calm:** Offers guided breathing sessions along with meditation and bedtime stories to help you unwind.
- **Headspace:** Includes breathing exercises as part of its focus on meditation and mindfulness practices.
- **Breathe2Relax:** Specifically tailored for managing stress, it walks you through deep breathing exercises to help you relax.

Using these apps regularly can really help you handle stress and anxiety better, which can make navigating the rollercoaster of teenage life a bit smoother.

Breathing techniques might seem simple, but they pack a powerful punch when it comes to shaping how you feel. They bring a sense of calm and clarity right when you need it most, even in the midst of all the craziness that comes with being a teen. Whether you're doing deep breathing, following rhythmic patterns, or using tech for guided exercises, getting a grip on your breath is like having a magic remote for your emotions. With just a few focused breaths, you can turn down the volume on stress and anxiety.

So, as you keep moving forward, keep in mind that every breath you take is a step toward feeling more balanced and at peace.

At the end of this book, you'll discover a Daily Breathing Challenge crafted just for you.

The Art of Mindfulness: Staying Present Amidst Chaos

Finding a moment of peace might seem like a far-off dream. But mindfulness is like a beacon in the storm, offering a path to tranquility and staying grounded in the present moment. It's all about being aware, moment by moment, of what's going on inside you and around you – your thoughts, feelings, sensations, and surroundings – with a gentle, caring perspective.

Mindfulness Explained

Mindfulness is all about observing without passing judgment. Whether you're noticing the rhythm of your breath, the beauty of a sunset, or the tension in your shoulders after a tough day, mindfulness encourages you to simply observe these experiences without labeling them as good or bad. This practice can change how you relate to your thoughts and emotions, ultimately improving your emotional well-being. It helps you see that thoughts and feelings come and go, like clouds drifting across the sky. This insight is key for dealing with stress and lessening the impact of negative emotions.

Mindfulness Practices

As you navigate the twists and turns of adolescence, integrating mindfulness into your daily life can be a powerful tool for emotional balance. Here are a few practices tailored just for you:

- **Mindful breathing:** Set aside a few minutes each day to focus entirely on your breath. Pay attention to the sensation of air entering and leaving your nostrils, the rise and fall of your chest, and the way your breath moves through your body.
- **Sensory awareness:** Pick one sense each day to concentrate on. It could be closely observing everything you see on your way to school or fully appreciating the flavors and textures of each bite during a meal. By tuning into your

senses, you develop a deeper connection to the present moment.

- **Body scan meditation:** Lie down and gradually shift your attention to different parts of your body, starting from your feet and working your way up to your head. Notice any sensations, tension, or discomfort, but don't try to change anything—just observe.

By practicing these exercises regularly, you can significantly reduce the distractions of external pressures and internal worries, allowing you to approach life with a calmer, more grounded perspective.

Reducing Anxiety Through Mindfulness

Anxiety, a common challenge, often feeds on worries about the past or future. Mindfulness helps by bringing your focus to the present moment, which naturally reduces anxiety's grip. A study in the *Journal of Clinical Psychiatry* found that mindfulness meditation can lessen anxiety symptoms by changing how the brain reacts to stress. By observing your thoughts and feelings without getting caught up in them, you gain the ability to face anxiety with greater understanding.

Mindfulness and School Stress

The pressures of school—academics, social dynamics, and future uncertainties—can create a lot of stress. Mindfulness offers a way to handle these challenges. Try the Pomodoro Technique during study sessions: work for 25 minutes, then take a 5-minute mindfulness or breathing break. This can boost your concentration and prevent burnout. Practicing mindful listening in class can not only improve your understanding but also make learning more engaging and enjoyable, transforming it from a stressful task into an interesting experience.

Incorporating mindfulness into your life doesn't require special equipment or a lot of time. It just needs a pause, a breath, and an open mind. Whether it's a few minutes of focused breathing, a mindful walk, or really listening to someone, mindfulness can help you navigate your busy life. It's not just a tool for coping with stress but for thriving amidst it.

Exercise as an Emotional Outlet: Moving Beyond Anxiety

When you're feeling super stressed and everything seems over-whelming, moving your body can really help. Working out or doing something active can release the built-up pressure inside. It's not just about getting sweaty or burning calories; it's about changing how you feel inside and giving you a break from all those worrying thoughts that come with anxiety.

Physical Activity and Emotional Health

Moving your body can really boost your mood. When you get active, it's not just your muscles that get a workout – your brain does, too. You don't have to do super intense workouts unless you like them. It's about finding fun ways to move. Maybe it's a dance class that feels more like a party, a yoga session that helps you breathe and relax, or a quick walk that clears your mind. The trick to sticking with exercise is finding activities you really enjoy. It's not about what you do, but about making sure it's something that excites you. Focusing on your body's movements helps you stay in the moment and forget your worries for a while. It's a great way to tell your brain, "Hey, let's just focus on this right now," and give yourself a break from feeling anxious.

Exercise and Brain Chemistry

The good feelings you get from exercise are all about brain chemistry. When you work out, your body releases endorphins, which are natural painkillers that make you feel good. But that's not all. Physical activity also increases dopamine, serotonin, and norepinephrine, which are chemicals that help control your mood. This process can help fight stress and make you feel happy and relaxed. It's like flipping a switch in your brain from tense to calm.

Creating a Routine

Sticking to a routine is crucial to get the emotional benefits of exercise. Here are some tips to make physical activity a regular part of your life:

- **Set realistic goals:** Start small and build up gradually. Even ten minutes a day can make a difference.
- **Plan ahead:** Schedule your workout sessions like any other appointment. This makes physical activity a non-negotiable part of your day.
- **Find a buddy:** Exercising with a friend can boost your motivation and make the activity more fun.
- **Track your progress:** Keep a log of your activities and note how you feel before and after. Seeing your progress can be a great motivator.
- **Be kind to yourself:** Some days you might not feel like exercising, and that's okay. Listen to your body and adjust as needed. The goal is to improve your mood, not add stress.

Incorporating exercise into your routine isn't just about getting fit; it's a powerful way to manage anxiety and stress. By finding activities you love, understanding how exercise affects your brain, and creating a routine that works for you, physical activity can become a cherished part of your day, giving you a break from worries and helping you feel good.

The Power of Music: Creating Your Emotional Playlist

Music has a unique way of touching your heart and moving your soul like nothing else. It's a universal language that speaks to you, changes your emotions, sets your mood, and even shifts your perspective on life. In this section, you'll learn how music can act as emotional therapy. I'll guide you through making mood-based playlists, explore how music and mindfulness work together, and show you how sharing music can deepen your connections with others.

Music as Emotional Therapy

Think about the last time a song made you feel something deep. Maybe it brought you joy, nostalgia, or a sense of calm. Music's ability to stir up such a range of emotions isn't by accident. Studies show that music can activate the same pleasure centers in your brain that respond to rewards like delicious food. But music's power goes beyond just feeling good; it can really shape your mood and emotional state. For example, classical music might calm you before a big test, while a strong rock anthem could get you hyped for a competition. This emotional impact is why music therapy is used to help manage stress, anxiety, and depression, making it easier for people to understand and handle their emotions.

Creating Mood-Based Playlists

Making playlists that match different moods can be a fun and effective way to use music for emotional balance. Here's how to start:

- **Categorize by emotion:** Think about the various moods you experience regularly. Common categories might include happiness, peace, motivation, or sadness.
- **Select songs intuitively:** Pick songs that naturally fit these moods for you. Trust your gut feeling on what belongs where.
- **Organize and refine:** Once you have a basic list, play through it. Adjust the order of the songs to create a flow that matches the emotional journey you want to experience.
- **Keep it dynamic:** Your emotional needs will change, and so should your playlists. Update them regularly with new songs or as your preferences evolve.

This personalized music collection will be your go-to resource for enhancing or shifting your mood whenever you need it.

Music and Mindfulness

Bringing music into mindfulness practices can boost the benefits of both. When you fully dive into the music, letting go of distractions, you're practicing mindfulness. Here are some ways to blend these practices:

- **Mindful listening:** Choose a piece of music and really listen to it. Pay attention to the instruments, rhythm, and how they interact. Notice your emotions and thoughts without judging them.
- **Meditation background:** Use instrumental or ambient music (like the violin, my personal favorite) during meditation. The right music can deepen your meditation, helping you feel calm and focused.
- **Breathing with music:** Find a song with a slow, steady rhythm and match your breathing to it. This can be calming, especially when you're feeling anxious or stressed.

Mixing music with mindfulness boosts your emotional well-being and helps you appreciate the music even more.

Sharing Music

Music has a special way of bringing people together like nothing else. Sharing music, whether it's swapping playlists, suggesting a song, or playing tunes at a get-together, can be a powerful way to express emotions and experiences that are hard to put into words.

- **Exchange playlists with friends:** It's a fun way to get to know each other better. You might find new music or see a different side of someone based on their taste.

- **Dedicate songs:** Sending someone a song that reminds you of them or a special time you shared can be a heartfelt gesture. It shows you're thinking of them and cherish your connection.
- **Group music discovery sessions:** Occasionally, gather with friends to share and listen to new discoveries or old favorites. These sessions spark interesting conversations and deepen understanding within the group.

Sharing music strengthens relationships and broadens musical horizons, enabling you to feel a wider range of emotions and understand different perspectives. Music, with its deep emotional impact, provides solace for the soul, healing for the heart, and a connection between minds. By purposefully including music in your life through mood-based playlists, combining it with mindfulness techniques, and sharing it with others, you unleash its complete power to transform, heal, and unite.

Time Management Tips: Reducing Stress by Taking Control

Feeling like there's never enough time in the day isn't just something adults deal with; it's something you face, too. Balancing homework, extracurriculars, socializing, and maybe even a part-time job can be overwhelming. But mastering time management can really ease the pressure, making you feel more in control and less like you're always scrambling to keep up.

How Time Management Affects Stress

How you handle your time can totally impact how stressed you feel. If you don't plan well and tasks start stacking up, stress is pretty much guaranteed to tag along. And let's be real, that stress isn't just a minor annoyance; it can mess with your ability to concentrate, sleep, and just generally feel good. But if you're good at managing your time, it's like having a superpower against stress. You'll feel more chill and in control, ready to take on tasks without them piling up and freaking you out.

Sorting Out What Matters Most

Knowing how to decide what stuff needs your attention first is key to being a time management champ. It's all about spotting the tasks that are both super important and need to be done ASAP and knocking those out first. One neat trick to help with this is the Eisenhower Box. It splits tasks into four groups:

- Do first (important and urgent).
- Schedule (important but not urgent).
- Delegate (urgent but not important).
- Delete (neither important nor urgent).

This handy tool can clear up what stuff needs to be done right away and what can chill for a bit.

- **Daily top three:** Every morning, pick out the three most important tasks for the day. Keeping your focus on these can stop your day from vanishing while you're caught up in small stuff.
- **The 80/20 rule:** Also called the Pareto Principle, this rule says that 80% of results come from just 20% of your efforts. Figuring out which tasks will make the biggest difference lets you put your energy where it really matters.

Tools and Apps for Time Management

Here are some cool tools and apps that can help you manage your time like a boss:

- **Trello:** Think of it like a digital whiteboard where you can organize your tasks into lists and cards. Super handy for seeing what needs to get done and tracking your progress on projects.

- **Google Keep:** This one's great for jotting down quick notes, setting reminders, and making checklists. It's simple and easy to use, perfect for keeping your thoughts in order.
- **Forest:** Need help staying focused? Forest has got your back. It's like a little game where you plant a virtual tree and it grows while you work. But if you get distracted and leave the app, your tree starts to wilt. It's a fun way to stay on track and avoid getting sucked into social media or texting.

Using these tools can keep your tasks organized and your mind clear, so you can say goodbye to the stress of trying to remember everything on your own.

Crafting a Daily Routine

Putting together a daily routine that mixes school stuff, hobbies, chill time, and hanging out with friends can seriously dial down the stress. Having a routine gives you a solid framework and makes everything feel more doable. Here's how to kick things off:

- **Sticking to a consistent sleep schedule:** Going to bed and waking up at the same time every day helps your body get into a rhythm, leading to better sleep and more energy during the day.
- **Setting study sessions:** Dedicate specific blocks of time each day to tackle homework and study sessions. This helps your brain get into study mode and also leaves room for relaxation.
- **Taking breaks:** Don't forget to give yourself short breaks throughout the day to recharge. Even just a quick walk or a few minutes of deep breathing can boost your productivity.
- **Adding fun and friend time:** Make sure your routine includes activities you enjoy and hanging out with friends.

It's important to balance work with play to avoid burning out.

As you wrap up this chapter, keep in mind that a well-crafted routine can turn your hectic day into a harmonious rhythm. Remember, mastering time management isn't just about ticking off tasks; it's about designing a life that feels purposeful and unhurried.

By grasping the connection between time and stress, learning to prioritize, harnessing digital tools, and establishing a balanced routine, you're laying the groundwork for a smoother, more successful journey ahead. These time management skills aren't just handy for your teen years; they'll guide you through adulthood, paving the way for a rich and balanced life.

3

CROSSING BRIDGES OF EMPATHY: CONNECTING WORLDS

"Empathy is about finding echoes of another person in yourself." – Mohsin Hamid

IMAGINE you're flipping through social media, and you stop on a post from a friend who's feeling low. You leave a nice comment right away. Have you ever thought about why you do that? It's because of empathy. You noticed they were sad, and you wanted to cheer them up. This chapter talks all about empathy—the thing that helps you understand and care for one another, making your friendships stronger.

Understanding Empathy

Empathy isn't just feeling sorry for someone. It's about putting yourself in their shoes and feeling what they feel. Think of empathy and sympathy as two sides of the same coin. Sympathy is like seeing someone stuck in a hole and offering them a ladder, while empathy is climbing down into the hole to sit with them. This shared emotional experience makes empathy super important for deep, meaningful friendships. It builds a connection based on mutual understanding and respect.

But here's the thing: empathy doesn't always come naturally. It's like a muscle that needs regular exercise to get stronger. The good news? There are ways to work on this empathy muscle, making it easier to connect with friends on a deeper level.

Empathy in Action

Seeing empathy in real life shows its power in friendships. Imagine your friend didn't make the team they tried out for. You've felt that kind of disappointment before. Using empathy, you remember those feelings, helping you connect with what your friend is going through. It's not just about saying, "That sucks," but sharing that you understand their disappointment and maybe even sharing how you coped with a similar situation.

Another example? Your friend is thrilled about acing a test. Empathy lets you share in their joy, truly feeling happy for them. It's celebrating their success as if it were your own, strengthening your bond, and reinforcing your friendship. My best friend, Kerrin, and I deeply empathize with each other. I feel incredible joy when something great happens in her life, and I also feel her pain during the tough times.

Challenges to Empathy

Even though understanding and sharing other people's feelings is awesome, it can be tough for teens like you. When everyone is trying to outdo each other or fighting for the same spot on a team or in a play, it's hard to be empathetic.

Social media doesn't make it any easier. It often shows just the good stuff, making it tricky to see what your friends are really going through. So, it feels more like you're comparing the best parts of your lives instead of sharing the real stuff.

But how can you overcome these obstacles? The first step is to start noticing them. Once you know these things are getting in the way, you can work on getting rid of them, making it easier to really connect with your friends through empathy.

Building Empathy Skills

Ready to strengthen your empathy muscle? Here are some practical exercises:

- **Perspective-taking:** Try to see things from your friend's point of view. Next time a friend shares something, pause and ask yourself, "How would I feel in their situation?" This shift in perspective can open your heart to deeper empathy.
- **Empathetic listening:** Listen to understand, not just to respond. When a friend is sharing, focus on their words and emotions. Nod, make eye contact, and repeat back a bit of what they said to show you're truly engaged.
- **Emotion labeling exercise:** When a friend is feeling down, work together to name the emotions they're experiencing. It might sound simple, but putting a name to an emotion can make it feel more manageable and less intimidating, fostering a deeper connection.
- **Empathy journal:** Keep a journal where you reflect on your daily interactions. Did you feel like you connected empathetically with your friends? Could you sense what they were feeling? Writing it down can help you become more aware of your empathetic responses and where you might need to grow.

Empathy isn't just about feeling for someone; it's about connecting in a way that words alone can't capture. It's what turns acquaintances into lifelong friends. By understanding empathy, recognizing it in action, overcoming its challenges, and actively building your empathy skills, you're not just becoming a better friend. You're also creating a world where people feel seen, heard, and valued. And in a world that often feels disconnected, that's a superpower worth having.

Active Listening: The Key to Truly Understanding Others

Hearing and active listening might sound the same, but they're totally different. Think about when you listen to your favorite song. Hearing is just the music going into your ears, but actively listening means you're really getting into the lyrics, feeling the emotions, and connecting with the heart of the song. That's the big difference: active listening means you're trying hard to not just hear the words, but to understand, think about, and react to the deeper meanings and feelings.

Active Listening Techniques

Becoming a great listener can really boost your relationships with others. Check out these tips to level up your active listening skills:

- **Pay attention to body language:** Your non-verbal cues say a lot. Keep eye contact, nod to show you're following along, and lean in a bit to show you're interested. These signals let the speaker know you're fully into the conversation. Disclaimer: If you're neurodivergent like me, sometimes you can't do multiple nonverbal cues at the same time, but take the time to figure out what you can achieve.
- **Hold back interruptions:** Give the speaker space to get their thoughts out without jumping in. This demonstrates that you value what they're saying and sets the stage for a more open discussion.
- **Paraphrase for clarity:** Summarize what you've heard in your own words to make sure you're on the same page. It

can be as simple as saying, "So, you're saying..." This helps clear up any misunderstandings and shows you're really trying to understand.

- **Ask open-ended questions:** Encourage more discussion by asking questions that need more than just a 'yes' or 'no' answer. This gets people thinking deeper and keeps the conversation flowing.
- **Give thoughtful feedback:** Show you're not just listening but also caring by giving feedback that's helpful and understanding. It lets the speaker know you're tuned into their feelings as well as their words.

Improving Your Listening Skills

Listening well can help you connect better with people, like your friends and family. Here are some easy ways to get better at it:

- **Talk time:** Use your everyday chats as practice sessions. Whether you're talking with a friend or a teacher, try to really pay attention to what they're saying.
- **Reflect:** After you've had a chat, take a moment to think about how it went. Did you understand everything? How did your responses affect the conversation?
- **Group chat:** Get together with friends and practice listening to each other. You can take turns talking about different topics while everyone else focuses on listening. It could be a club or just a hangout where you all try to improve your listening skills together.

Active Listening in Digital Conversations

Talking online has its own set of challenges and perks. Without seeing someone's face or hearing their voice, it can be tricky to understand their feelings. Here are some tips to help you listen better in digital chats:

- **Take your time:** It's tempting to reply quickly, but take a moment to really read the message first.
- **Show you care with words:** Since you can't use body language, choose words that show empathy. Say things like, "I can imagine how that must feel" or "It sounds like you're really into this" to show you understand.
- **Ask and repeat:** If something isn't clear, don't be afraid to ask questions or repeat what you think the other person means. This helps avoid misunderstandings.
- **Use emojis and GIFs:** While they aren't a perfect substitute for real emotions, emojis, and GIFs can help show how you feel and make the conversation warmer.

Whether you're talking face-to-face or online, good listening is key to better relationships. When you truly listen, you make your own life better and brighten the lives of those around you, building connections based on a deeper level of care and understanding.

Dealing with Peer Pressure Using Emotional Intelligence

During your teen years, you'll likely face the tricky challenge of peer pressure. This is when friends or classmates try to get you to do things that might not match your values or make you uncomfortable. The first step to standing up for yourself is understanding the different types of peer pressure. Emotional intelligence (EQ) gives you the skills to handle these situations and stay true to yourself.

Identifying Peer Pressure

Peer pressure doesn't always come with a neon sign. Sure, it can be as blatant as a friend daring you to skip class. But often, it's more subtle, like a nudge to conform to the group's dress code or laugh along at a joke you find offensive. It might even disguise itself as persuasion—"Come on, everyone's trying it"—masking the underlying pressure. Keeping an eye out for these variations helps you stay one step ahead, ready to respond in ways that respect your boundaries.

Emotional Intelligence as Your Shield

Think of emotional intelligence as your personal shield against peer pressure. It starts with self-awareness—knowing your values, limits, and how different situations make you feel. This understanding is your first defense, helping you see when peer pressure is happening and why it affects you.

Next, emotional intelligence is about managing your feelings, especially when peer pressure makes you scared, anxious, or eager to fit in. By recognizing these emotions without letting them control you, you can make choices that reflect who you truly are, not just what others expect.

Social awareness, another part of emotional intelligence, helps you read the room. Is the pressure coming from one person or the whole group? Are others feeling the same way you are? This awareness can help you respond wisely, showing empathy for yourself and others.

Finally, relationship management is key. It's about standing up for yourself without causing conflict. With emotional intelligence, you can communicate your decisions in a way that keeps respect and understanding on both sides.

Confidence and Assertiveness

Building confidence and assertiveness is key to resisting peer pressure. When you have confidence rooted in a strong sense of self, it helps you stand firm in your decisions. It's that inner voice saying, "You know what's best for you," even when others are trying to tell you otherwise.

Assertiveness is confidence in action. It's the ability to express your thoughts and feelings openly and respectfully. Here's how you can develop it:

- **Practice saying no:** Start with small, low-stakes situations. Each time you say "no," you strengthen your assertiveness muscle, getting ready for bigger challenges.
- **Use "I" statements:** Frame your responses from your perspective to avoid sounding accusatory. For example, say "I feel uncomfortable with this," instead of "You're wrong to ask me."
- **Role-play scenarios:** With a trusted friend or in front of a mirror, practice how you'd respond to different forms of peer pressure. This practice can boost your confidence for when you face the real thing.

Peer Support Systems

Building a support system is like creating your own cheer squad that helps you stay true to yourself. This squad can be made up of friends who get you, mentors, family, or anyone who respects your choices. Here's how a strong support system can help you deal with peer pressure:

- **Strength in numbers:** It's easier to stand up to peer pressure when you know you're not alone. Having friends who support you makes a big difference.
- **A place to talk:** Sometimes, you just need to talk things out. A support system gives you a safe space to share your thoughts and feelings.
- **Role models:** Friends or mentors who handle peer pressure well can inspire you. Their experiences can teach you how to deal with similar situations.

Facing peer pressure with emotional intelligence isn't about building a tough shield around yourself. It's about knowing yourself well enough to act in ways that reflect your true self, even when others try to influence you. It's about finding a balance between being open to others and staying true to yourself. And most importantly, it's about having a circle of support that gives you the courage to be yourself, no matter what.

The Impact of Kindness: Small Acts, Big Changes

With so much news about arguments and disagreements, kindness might seem too small to matter. But in reality, kindness stands out, bringing people together and making everything warmer. For someone like you, figuring out life and choosing to be kind not only helps others but also makes you feel better inside. It's all about realizing that even the smallest kind act can lead to big, positive changes.

Kindness and Emotional Health

Kindness is awesome because it helps both the giver and the receiver. When you do something kind for someone, it doesn't just make their day better—it makes you feel good, too. This is called the "helper's high," and it's all about biology. Kind acts release feel-good hormones like dopamine and oxytocin, which boost your mood and make you feel more connected to others. At your age, when figuring out who you are and building relationships is super important, being kind can make you feel more confident and like you belong. It shows you that you have the power to make a positive impact, and that's a pretty cool thing to realize.

Random Acts of Kindness

Adding kindness to your daily life doesn't need to be a big deal. It's the small acts that often make the biggest impact and are most remembered. Here are a few simple ways to sprinkle kindness throughout your day:

- **Compliment a friend:** Notice something you genuinely admire or appreciate about a friend and tell them.

It could be as simple as praising their sense of humor or a recent accomplishment.

- **Help out at home:** Offer to do a chore without being asked. It could be anything from washing the dishes to helping a sibling with their homework.
- **Pay it forward:** Next time you're at a café, consider paying for the person in line behind you. It's a small gesture that can unexpectedly brighten someone's day.
- **Leave a positive note:** Write a cheerful message on a sticky note and leave it somewhere it'll be found, like inside a library book or on a restroom mirror.

Kindness in the Digital World

The online world, where it's easy to hide behind screens and say hurtful things, really needs kindness. As someone who grew up in the digital age, you have a special chance to make online interactions more positive. Here are some ways to spread kindness online:

- **Spread positivity in comments:** Use your online presence to lift others up. Leave nice comments on your friends' posts or offer supportive words to someone having a hard time.
- **Share uplifting content:** Share quotes, stories, or videos that spread hope and encouragement. Your posts can be like a little beam of light for someone who needs it.
- **Stand against cyberbullying:** If you see someone being bullied online, speak out. Show support to the person being bullied and report the behavior. Standing together against cyberbullying can make a big difference.

At the end of this book, you'll discover an Empathy Activation Challenge designed just for you.

The Ripple Effect

One of the coolest things about kindness is how it can spread like ripples in a pond. Each act of kindness has the power to inspire others to do the same, creating a chain reaction that can touch lots of lives. And this isn't just wishful thinking—it's backed up by research. Studies show that seeing acts of kindness makes people more likely to be kind themselves in the future.

For you, this means that even the smallest acts of kindness can help create a world where empathy and understanding are the norm. Imagine a school where students regularly compliment each other, help out with notes or study tips without thinking twice, and support each other online with encouragement. This isn't some far-off dream; it's totally doable, one act of kindness at a time.

By choosing kindness, you're joining a team of people making the world a better place. It shows that even in a world that sometimes feels all about me-me-me, connection and caring about others can bring us closer together. With each small act of kindness, you're not just brightening someone else's day; you're starting a movement that builds a more understanding and connected community, one act at a time.

From Online Friends to Real Connections: Bridging the Digital Gap

In today's digital age, making friends is just a click away, blurring the lines between online and offline worlds. Online friendships, born from shared interests or mutual connections on social media, are truly valuable. They provide companionship, support, and a sense of belonging, often overcoming geographical barriers that physical friendships may struggle with. These digital connections can be just as genuine and meaningful as those formed in person, whether in the classroom or on the playground.

However, nurturing friendships solely in the digital realm comes with its own challenges. Without physical presence, emotional exchanges can lose some of their depth, leading to more misunderstandings. The absence of non-verbal cues makes it easier for messages to be misinterpreted, resulting in unnecessary conflicts. And the convenience of online connectivity sometimes leads to surface-level interactions, where meaningful conversations struggle to take root. Recognizing these obstacles is the first step toward building stronger bonds.

Transitioning online friendships into real-life connections offers a way to tackle some of these challenges. Here are a few tips for those seeking to bridge the gap:

- **Safety first:** When planning to meet an online friend in person, safety should be your top priority. Always arrange to meet in public spaces, and consider bringing along a trusted friend or family member for added security.
- **Shared experiences:** Look for activities that you both enjoy to make your meet-up more enjoyable. Whether it's attending a concert of a favorite band or visiting a museum featuring art you've discussed online, shared experiences can help strengthen your bond.
- **Open and honest communication:** Don't hesitate to share your feelings about the meet-up. It's completely normal to feel nervous or unsure, and being open about these feelings can help both parties manage their expectations.
- **Give it time:** Keep in mind that the dynamics of in-person interactions may feel different than those online. Give yourselves time to adjust to this new mode of friendship and allow your connection to grow naturally.

Finding the right balance between online and face-to-face interactions is crucial for nurturing these friendships. Here are some strategies:

- **Regular check-ins:** Make time for both online and offline interactions. Schedule regular video chats or plan monthly meet-ups if possible, considering geographical distances and safety measures.
- **Digital detoxes:** Encourage periods where you both disconnect from social media and technology to focus on real-life connections. This break can deepen your bond and make your time together more meaningful.
- **Communicate across platforms:** Mix up your communication methods. Use texts and social media for quick updates, but also make time for phone calls or video chats for more personal interactions.
- **Foster other interests:** Support each other in pursuing hobbies or interests outside of the digital world. This not only adds depth to your individual lives but also brings new topics to your conversations and interactions.

Navigating the complexities of online friendships isn't about downplaying their worth but about enhancing them into tangible bonds. It's about striking the right balance between virtual and face-to-face experiences, ensuring that the friendship flourishes in every dimension.

As we conclude this exploration of empathy, active listening, handling peer pressure with emotional intelligence, the transformative impact of kindness, and the transition from online friendships to real connections, it's evident that these aspects are interlinked. Each plays a pivotal role in shaping healthy, enriching relationships. As you move forward, carry these insights with you, utilizing them to nurture connections that are deep, meaningful, and resilient in the face of life's challenges.

4

CONVERSING WINDS: CRAFTING CONNECTIONS THROUGH WORDS

"Words are, in my not-so-humble opinion, our most inexhaustible source of magic." – J.K. Rowling

IMAGINE you're in front of a huge forest where every tree stands for a thought, feeling, or something you want to say but find it hard to. Now, picture yourself discovering a way through this thick forest. This path isn't made of rocks or grass, but of the words you use. They're like stepping stones helping you communicate better and understand others more. This chapter acts as your guide through this journey. It shows you how the words you pick, the way you say them, and the situation you're in all play a big role in shaping your world and your connections with others.

The Power of Words: Communicating with Clarity and
Compassion

Making a Difference through Communication

Words hold a lot of power. They have the ability to heal a wounded
soul or crush someone's confidence. Think back to a moment when
someone's words made you feel better or, on the flip side, made you
feel worse. It's not just about what you say, but how you say it that
really sticks with people. Take a look at the difference between saying
"You never understand me!" and "Sometimes, I feel like you don't get
where I'm coming from." The first one blames and pushes people
away, while the second one shares a personal feeling, opening up a
chance for understanding rather than conflict.

Expressing Your Needs and Feelings

Sharing your needs and feelings openly and honestly can sometimes
feel like walking on a tightrope without any safety net. It's all about
finding balance. On one side, there's the raw truth of what you're
going through, and on the other, there's the vulnerability of opening
up about it. Here's a trick to help keep that balance: use "I" statements
(sound familiar?). Instead of saying, "You make me angry," try saying,
"I feel angry when..." This small change puts the focus on your own
experience rather than blaming someone else, making room for a
more positive conversation.

- **Exercise:** Think about a recent situation where you felt
  like you weren't understood or listened to. Write down what
  you wanted to say, and then rewrite it using "I" statements.
  Notice if there's any difference in how the message comes
  across.

The Importance of Tone and Context

Words can vary greatly depending on the tone and context in which they're used. Saying "I'm fine" with a smile can show happiness, but saying the same words with a sigh might suggest feeling down. Context is also key. A joke shared with close pals might not be suitable in a formal setting. Paying attention to both tone and context ensures your message comes across as you intend, promoting understanding and respect.

- **Reflection:** Recall a time when someone misunderstood what you meant. How did tone or context contribute to this? How could you adjust these factors in future conversations?

Empathetic Communication

Think of empathy in communication like a bridge connecting two distant shores. It's not just about understanding where someone else is coming from; it's about letting them know they're truly seen and heard. One way to practice this kind of communication is through active listening, which we talked about in Chapter 3. When someone shares something with you, really focus on what they're saying. Try not to plan your response while they're talking, and repeat back to them what you've understood. This simple act can make them feel validated and strengthen your connection.

- **Try this:** Next time you're chatting with someone, challenge yourself to listen deeply. After they've finished speaking, reflect on what they've said by saying something like, "It seems like you're feeling..." or "So, if I understand correctly, you're saying..." Notice how this openness changes the dynamic of your conversation.

Words have the power to either build bridges or put up walls. How you use them is up to you. As you navigate the ups and downs of being a teen, embracing clear and compassionate communication can lead to deeper relationships and a better understanding of both yourself and those around you. It's not just about talking; it's about connecting, understanding, and ultimately building relationships that are meaningful, resilient, and fulfilling.

Navigating Tough Talks with Confidence

Difficult conversations are bound to happen, especially during your teenage years when emotions are intense, and relationships are constantly changing. Whether it's clearing up a misunderstanding with a friend, addressing hurtful behavior with someone, or talking about a sensitive issue with your parents, these talks need a mix of honesty, empathy, and resilience. Here's how to tackle them with confidence, making sure they end positively instead of adding to the conflict.

Preparing for Tough Talks

The key to handling any challenging conversation well is preparation, especially when the stakes are high. Start by sorting out your thoughts and feelings. Write down what you want to say, focusing on the main points you want to get across. This helps you organize your thoughts and gives you a chance to think about what you truly feel and why.

Next, try to imagine how the other person might react. Put yourself in their shoes and think about possible responses. You don't need to plan out every word of the conversation, but having a clear idea of your message and potential reactions can help you stay on track and keep calm.

- **Set a goal for the conversation:** Decide what you want to achieve. Is it understanding, an apology, a change in behavior, or simply expressing your feelings? Having a clear purpose can shape how the conversation unfolds.
- **Choose the right time and place:** Timing matters. Look for a moment when both of you are relatively calm and not dealing with other stressful things. Find a private, neutral space where you won't be interrupted.

Staying Calm and Focused

Keeping your cool during a tough conversation isn't easy, but it's important. Not only does it help you communicate better, but it also encourages the other person to listen and respond thoughtfully. Here are some techniques:

- **Breathe:** Before you jump in, take a few deep breaths. It might seem simple, but it can really help ease tension and keep you calm.
- **Pause before responding:** If you feel your emotions starting to rise, take a moment to breathe and gather your thoughts. It's totally okay to say, "I need a moment," to make sure your response is thoughtful and measured.
- **Keep a positive outlook:** Remind yourself that the aim here is to solve the problem and strengthen your relationship, not to come out on top in an argument. Hold onto that mindset as you navigate the conversation.

Conflict Resolution Skills

Effective conflict resolution can turn a potentially damaging situation into an opportunity for growth and understanding. Here are some tools to navigate disagreements constructively:

- **Listen actively:** Show genuine interest in the other person's perspective. Make eye contact, nod to acknowledge their points, and reflect back on what you've heard to ensure understanding. (This isn't new at this point, right? You got this!)
- **Use "I" statements:** Express your feelings and needs without blaming the other person. For instance, say, "I feel upset when..." instead of "You make me upset by..." (Again, I can't emphasize this enough!)
- **Seek common ground:** Find areas of agreement and build on them. This can lay the groundwork for finding a solution that works for both parties.
- **Agree to disagree:** Sometimes, reaching a complete agreement isn't possible. Acknowledge and respect your differences as a positive step forward.

Learning from Tough Talks

Every tricky chat teaches us something valuable, whether it's about how we talk, what sets us off, or how we relate to someone. Take a moment to think about what went okay and what could've been better. Maybe try jotting down:

- **How you felt before, during, and after the talk:** It might show you when you're likely to get upset and help you do better next time.
- **What actually happened during the chat:** Did you get what you wanted? Did anything change afterward?
- **What you learned about yourself and the other person:** Understanding each other's views can make your bond stronger and help you chat better later on.

Thinking of tough talks as chances to grow and connect can make them less scary. If you come prepared, show empathy, and bounce back from tough moments, you can turn them into opportunities to build stronger, more real friendships.

Saying No: Setting Healthy Limits with Emotional Intelligence

Think of boundaries like your personal guidelines. They show what's cool and what's not cool for you. Boundaries are super important because they keep you in check, making sure you don't spread yourself too thin or let people treat you in ways that don't sit right with you. Without them, your relationships can start to feel more draining than fulfilling.

But setting boundaries isn't just about putting distance between you and others. It's about carving out a safe space where your relationships can grow strong. It's realizing that to respect others, you have to respect yourself first. Understanding this is the first step to knowing when to say no.

Why Boundaries Are Important

Imagine a garden without a fence. Anything or anyone could stroll in, messing up the flowers and causing chaos. Boundaries act like that fence, letting good things stay in and keeping the bad stuff out. They help you:

- Preserve your mental and emotional energy
- Protect your self-esteem
- Nurture respect in your relationships

Crafting Your No

Saying no can feel tricky, especially if you're worried about how the other person will react. But it's a skill you can get better at, allowing you to stay true to yourself while still being respectful. Here's how:

- Start with gratitude. Show appreciation for the request. "Thanks for thinking of me for this..."
- Be clear but kind. Don't beat around the bush if you mean no. "I'm sorry, I can't commit to that right now..."
- Offer an alternative if you can. "I can't help with X, but maybe you could try..."
- Keep it short and sweet. You don't need a long explanation, and remember, "no" is a complete sentence, thought, and statement.

Dealing with Pushback

When you set boundaries, not everyone will respect them right away. Some might challenge you, seeing if you'll budge. Here's how to handle it:

- Stay steady but cool. Repeat your boundary calmly, using the same clear and polite words.
- Avoid getting into debates. Your boundaries don't need explaining.
- Know when to step back. If someone keeps disrespecting your boundaries, it might be worth rethinking the relationship.

Boundaries: A Sign of Self-Respect

Every time you draw a line, you're saying something big about yourself. You're showing you care about your well-being, your time, and your emotions. This self-respect not only makes life better for you but also sets a standard for how others should treat you. Keep in mind:

- It's totally fine to put yourself first sometimes.
- Saying no doesn't mean you're selfish or mean.
- Boundaries make for deeper, realer connections with others.

Setting boundaries isn't a one-time thing. It's a journey of checking in with yourself and figuring out what's right for you. It's about finding a balance where your needs and others' needs fit together smoothly. And by doing that, you build relationships based on respect and understanding, where everyone's boundaries matter.

Understanding Non-Verbal Cues in Yourself and Others

Words are powerful, but so are gestures, expressions, and how we carry ourselves. This silent language of body signals tells a lot about how we feel, what we mean, and how we react, both to ourselves and to others. Paying attention to these non-verbal cues can really boost your understanding and make your communication way stronger.

The Language of Body Signals

Body language covers all the ways you communicate without speaking a word. It's about facial expressions, gestures, how you stand or sit, and even how close you are to someone else. For example, crossed arms might show you're feeling defensive or uneasy, while a real smile can show you're warm and open. Learning to read these signals can really change how you interact with people, helping you respond with more understanding and effectiveness.

- **Try this:** Spend a day watching how people use their body language. See how it matches up with what they're saying, or if it tells you something different. Think about what that tells you about how they're feeling and what they're thinking.

Being Aware of Your Own Body Signals

Just like you pick up on others' non-verbal cues, they're doing the same with you. Being aware of the signals you're sending can help you make sure your body language matches what you mean. For instance, if you want to show you're paying attention but you keep looking at your phone, your body language says otherwise. Checking in with yourself during conversations to make sure your posture, facial expressions, and gestures show you're engaged and empathetic can really change how people see and understand you.

- **Try this:** Stand in front of a mirror and think about different emotions—like happiness, anger, sadness, and excitement. Practice showing these emotions only through your face and how you stand. This can help you notice how you might be unconsciously sharing your feelings through your body language.

Misunderstandings and Cultural Diversity

Non-verbal signals aren't the same everywhere; cultural differences can really change what they mean. For instance, in some places, looking someone in the eye is a sign of respect, but in others, it might seem confrontational. And gestures that are totally fine in one culture might be offensive in another. Being aware of these differences matters, especially in our world where cultures mix more than ever. It's about respecting different ways of doing things and not assuming everyone sees things the same way you do.

- **Try this:** Look into the body language norms of a culture different from yours. Pay attention to gestures or actions that are really different from what you're used to. Think about how these differences could affect communication between different cultures.

Understanding the subtle but important world of non-verbal communication takes time, watching, and practice. By paying attention to the silent messages you and others send, you can build stronger connections and have more meaningful conversations. It's a process of learning and adjusting, but it makes you better at communicating and connecting with people from all walks of life.

At the end of this book, you'll discover a Mindful Posting Challenge tailored just for you.

YOUR THOUGHTS MATTER!

Your feedback doesn't just help future readers, but also guides me in creating an even more impactful book. Your insights can empower other teens and parents, helping them make informed decisions. Your perspective might just resonate with someone else's situation, giving them the confidence to start their own journey of self-discovery and growth.

5

SCALING MOUNTAINS OF ADVERSITY: CULTIVATING RESILIENCE

"Technology should improve your life, not become your life." – Billy Cox

THE JOURNEY to success isn't a smooth path; it's more like a hike up a mountain. There are highs and lows, twists and turns, and sometimes, you hit a dead end. But every challenge, every setback, can be a stepping stone toward your goals. This chapter isn't about dodging failure because, let's be real, it's a part of life. It's about learning to see failure differently, as a chance to get back up stronger and smarter.

Turning Failure into a Stepping Stone for Success

Understanding Failure as Part of Learning

Once you understand that failure isn't the opposite of success but part of it, everything changes. Think about learning to ride a bike.

Nobody jumps on a bike for the first time and just takes off. There are wobbles and falls. But those falls teach you balance and control. Suddenly, what seemed scary becomes manageable. The same goes for any skill or goal in life. Failure isn't a sign to give up; it's feedback, a nudge to adjust and try again with more insight.

- **Real-life example:** Imagine a student who fails a math test. Instead of seeing it as a blow to their intelligence, they can view it as a signal to change their study habits or get extra help. The next test then becomes a chance to use these new strategies, turning a past failure into a step toward improvement.

Reframing Your Perspective on Failure

Changing how you view failure isn't easy; it takes practice and patience. Start with these techniques:

- **Label the experience, not yourself:** Instead of saying, "I'm a failure," say, "I failed at this task." This small change in language makes a big difference, keeping your self-esteem separate from the event.
- **Seek the lesson:** After a setback, ask yourself, "What can I learn from this?" This approach shifts your focus from dwelling on the failure to discovering how you can grow because of it.
- **Visualize a different outcome:** Imagine facing a similar challenge but succeeding. What did you do differently in your visualization? This can help you identify changes you can make in real life.

Success Stories

History is full of people who faced setbacks but didn't let them define their paths. Take Thomas Edison, for example. His journey to invent the lightbulb involved thousands of unsuccessful attempts. Yet, he famously said, "I have not failed. I've just found 10,000 ways that won't work." Each "failure" brought him closer to his groundbreaking invention. Stories like Edison's remind us that perseverance in the face of adversity can lead to amazing achievements. You might even follow an influencer on social media who shares their journey from failure to success, showing that setbacks are just steps on the road to success.

Cultivating a Positive Response to Failure

Developing a constructive response to failure is key to turning setbacks into opportunities for growth. Here are some strategies:

- **Practice self-compassion:** Treat yourself with the same kindness you would offer a friend in your situation. Acknowledge the disappointment but avoid harsh self-criticism.
- **Analyze the experience:** Break down what happened and why. This analysis can uncover valuable insights to guide your next steps.
- **Set small, achievable goals:** After a setback, setting and achieving small goals can rebuild your confidence and momentum.

Bullet points for a positive response checklist:

- Did I treat myself kindly?
- What did I learn from this experience?
- What's one small step I can take right now toward my goal?

When you look at failure with a mindset focused on growth, it changes from being a barrier to being a push for personal growth. Think of each mistake not as a dead end but as a sign to try a different route, maybe one you never thought of before. This way of thinking helps not just with big life goals but also with everyday problems, making it a great tool for building strength and growing.

The Role of Feedback: Growing from Criticism

Handling feedback and criticism is like learning a new dance. At first, it feels awkward, and you might make a few mistakes. But with time, you get the hang of it. Learning to tell the difference between helpful and hurtful feedback is a key part of this dance, turning possible mistakes into smooth moves forward.

Differentiating Constructive from Destructive Feedback

Imagine you're painting a picture. Constructive feedback is like someone suggesting a different shade of blue for the sky to make your painting stand out. Destructive feedback is like someone saying your sky ruins the whole picture without explaining why or how you could make it better.

- **Look for specifics:** Constructive criticism offers clear advice on what could be better and why. It's something you can act on.
- **Tone matters:** Even well-meant feedback can seem harsh if the tone is rude.
- **Respectful delivery:** Constructive criticism is given in a way that respects your feelings.
- **Focus on the work:** If the feedback attacks you personally, it's not constructive. Good feedback targets your work or behavior, not your character.

Understanding these differences helps you filter criticism, keeping what helps you grow and letting go of what doesn't. This may take some time before getting the hang of this skill, but you can do it!

· · ·

Receiving Feedback with Grace

Hearing that your efforts fell short can sting, no doubt. But embracing feedback is about looking past that initial discomfort and seeing the chance to learn and get better. Here's how to accept feedback without letting it bring you down:

- **Breathe and listen:** Before reacting, take a deep breath. Listen fully to what's being said without planning your response.
- **Thank them:** A simple "Thank you for your feedback" shows you appreciate their effort to help you improve, even if you don't agree with everything.
- **Ask for examples:** If the feedback isn't clear, ask for specific examples. This shows you genuinely want to understand and improve.
- **Give yourself time:** If the feedback is tough to take, give yourself time to process it. Reflect on it later when you can be more objective.

Using Feedback for Personal Growth

Feedback, especially the helpful kind, is like a treasure trove for your personal and academic improvement. It shines a light on areas you might have missed and gives you a fresh view of your work or actions. Here's how to make feedback work for you:

- **Identify the main message:** Break down the feedback to its most important points. What's the key thing to take away?
- **Make a plan:** Based on the feedback, list specific steps you can take to get better. For example, if someone says you need stronger thesis statements in essays, your plan could involve studying good examples or joining a writing workshop.

- **Find resources:** Sometimes, improving means learning new stuff. Don't be afraid to look for help, like books, online classes, or advice from people you trust.
- **Track your progress:** Keep a record of the feedback you get and what you're doing about it. Over time, you'll see how you've grown and how feedback has helped.

Turning feedback into a growth tool not only boosts your skills but also makes you stronger. You learn to bounce back even better after setbacks, armed with new ideas and plans.

Building Openness to Feedback

Getting comfortable with feedback takes time. It starts with changing how you think about it – seeing feedback as a chance to grow, not something scary. Try these exercises to help you get there:

- **Feedback reflection journal:** After you get feedback, write down how you feel about it, whether you think it's helpful, and how you plan to use it. Doing this can make criticism feel less harsh and more useful.
- **Role-play receiving feedback:** Practice getting feedback from a friend or family member. They can pretend to give you both helpful and not-so-helpful feedback. Practice staying calm and responding in a positive way.
- **Feedback swap:** Team up with a classmate or coworker to give each other feedback regularly. This way, feedback becomes a normal part of improving together. These exercises can make feedback feel less scary and more like a tool for getting better.

Feedback is like a guiding light. It shows you ways to improve that you might miss on your own. Learning to tell helpful feedback from hurtful feedback, accepting it gracefully, using it to grow, and being open to it are all steps in a dance toward getting better in school and in life. Each time you get feedback, you're not just learning about your work; you're learning about yourself too, getting better at handling challenges and making changes.

Building Your Personal Resilience Toolbox

Identifying Your Inner Strengths

Finding and nurturing your inner strengths is like uncovering hidden treasures within yourself. Once you find them, they become your allies when life gets tough. Here's how to begin:

1. Try a strengths-finding activity to discover what you're naturally good at.
2. Get a journal and write down times when you felt really good or accomplished.
3. Think about these moments and figure out what qualities helped you achieve them.

Maybe you've shown creativity in solving a problem, determination in studying for an exam, or kindness in helping a friend. Recognizing these strengths is the first step to using them more often in your daily life.

- **Strengths spotting:** Ask friends or family to tell you what they think your strengths are. They might notice things about you that you haven't seen.
- **Play to your strengths:** Try to use your strengths in new ways. For example, if you're good at solving problems, look for chances to use your creative thinking in projects you volunteer for.

Building a Strong Support System

The people around you can be your biggest support, cheering you on, giving advice, and listening when you need to talk. To start building this support network, reach out and be open to making connections. Join clubs, groups, or teams that share your interests; these can be great places to meet people who understand you. Also, consider finding a mentor. A mentor is someone who can guide you, share their experiences, and help you through tough times. Your mentor could be a teacher, coach, older sibling, or family friend.

- **Keeping in touch:** Make a habit of catching up with friends or mentors regularly. These chats don't always have to be about getting advice; just chatting about your day can strengthen your relationship.
- **Give and receive support:** Remember, supporting each other works both ways. Be there for your friends and mentors, offering help and encouragement when they need it. This mutual care builds a strong bond of respect and trust.

Taking Care of Yourself

Looking after yourself is super important for staying strong, but it often gets pushed aside when life gets hectic (we'll dive deeper into this in Chapter 8). It's not just about physical health; it's also about looking after your feelings and thoughts. Start small. Make sure you're getting enough sleep, eating good food, and keeping active. But don't forget to do stuff that makes you happy and chilled out, like reading, painting, or hanging with pals. And remember, looking after yourself isn't selfish; it's what keeps you ready to tackle whatever life throws at you.

- **Self-care stuff:** Make a list of things that help you relax or feel better, like a "self-care menu." When you need a boost, pick something from your list that fits how you're feeling.

- **Take a break from screens:** Think about taking some time each week to switch off from all your devices. This break can lower stress and help you focus better, plus you might sleep better, too.

Building your personal resilience toolbox is something you work on over time. It means finding out what you're good at, figuring out how to handle your feelings, building up a network of people who've got your back, and looking after yourself. These tools help you deal with tough stuff and come out the other side even tougher, smarter, and closer to yourself and the people you care about.

Finding the Good in Every Experience

Life brings a mix of ups and downs – some awesome moments and others that really test you. It's natural to want to remember the good stuff and forget the tough times. But actually, it's often when things don't go to plan that you learn the most important stuff.

Learning from Mistakes

Making mistakes is totally normal. They happen when you try new stuff or push yourself out of your comfort zone. But here's the cool part: mistakes are like a treasure trove of knowledge. The trick is to see them not as failures, much like constructive feedback, but as chances to learn and grow. Here's how you can squeeze the wisdom out of every slip-up:

- **Take a breather:** When you mess up, give yourself a moment to chill. This helps you calm down and look at what happened without all the emotions getting in the way.
- **Figure out what went wrong:** Pinpoint exactly where things didn't go to plan. Was it a bad decision, not enough

info, or maybe you forgot to plan something? Knowing what caused the mess-up is the first step to learning from it.

- **Use what you've learned:** Now that you know what went wrong, think about how you can do things differently next time. Maybe you need to change your approach, do more research, or try a new tactic.

This process turns every mistake into a stepping stone, gradually building a path toward your goals lined with the wisdom of experiences past.

The Power of Reflection

Reflective practices, such as journaling, offer a structured way to sift through your experiences, extracting lessons and insights that might otherwise go unnoticed. Here's how to incorporate reflection into your daily routine:

- **Set aside time for reflection:** Dedicate a few minutes each day to reflect on your experiences. It could be in the morning, setting the tone for the day ahead, or in the evening, looking back on the day's events.
- **Use prompts to guide your reflection:** If you're unsure where to start, use prompts like "What challenged me today?" or "What did I learn about myself?" These questions can help direct your focus toward learning opportunities.
- **Review your reflections:** Periodically, look back on your past entries. You'll often find patterns in your experiences and the lessons they've taught you, offering valuable insights into your growth journey.

Reflection turns experiences into lessons, ensuring that no challenge or mistake goes by without contributing to your personal development.

Embracing Change

Change happens all the time, even though it can feel kinda scary. But here's the thing: being open to change can lead to some really cool stuff and help you grow big time. Here's how to get comfy with change:

- **Feel your feelings:** It's totally okay to feel nervous or scared when things change. Just acknowledging those feelings is the first step to dealing with them.
- **Find the good stuff:** Every change brings new stuff to explore. Try focusing on the good bits – like new things to learn, new friends to make, and new adventures to have.
- **Take it step by step:** Big changes can feel like a lot to handle. Try breaking them down into smaller bits. It makes adjusting to change feel less scary and more doable.

Just remember, when you're cool with change, it can help you grow loads, pushing you to try new stuff and discover awesome things you never knew were possible.

Staying Curious

Curiosity is like the fuel that keeps your brain running and growing. It's what makes you want to ask questions, find answers, and dive into new stuff. Here's how to keep that curiosity fire burning:

- **Try new things:** Give yourself the green light to check out things you've never tried before. Who knows? You might stumble upon something you love that you never knew about.
- **Ask away:** Get in the habit of asking questions, whether it's to yourself or other people. Questions are like keys that unlock all sorts of cool knowledge and understanding.

- **Question everything:** Your assumptions can be sneaky and hold you back. Try poking holes in them – it can lead to all kinds of new ideas and ways of thinking.

Being curious makes life feel like a never-ending adventure, where every day brings something new to learn. It keeps you moving forward, always growing and changing as you go.

Resilience Stories: Teens Like You, Getting Stronger

Life throws all sorts of stuff at teenagers, right? Everyone's got their own mix of challenges, just like everyone's different. These stories show how teens like you deal with tough stuff, from school stress to tough times at home. They're all about bouncing back and growing stronger. When you read them, you might see a bit of yourself – and realize just how strong you can be, too.

Real-Life Examples

- **Jaxon's academic journey:** Jaxon had a tough time with reading and writing because he has dyslexia. It made schoolwork really hard. But instead of giving up, Jaxon tackled his learning difference head-on. With some cool strategies and a whole lot of determination, he got way better, and guess what? He even won a big writing contest! Jaxon's story shows that struggles in school don't have to hold you back.
- **Ava's healing journey:** When Ava lost a parent at 16, it felt like her whole world fell apart. Dealing with the sadness was super tough. But over time, with help from friends and by doing things that reminded her of her parent, Ava found a way to carry on. She learned that even though the pain never goes away, it becomes part of who you are. Ava's story

proves that even in the hardest times, there's room for growth and strength.

- **Cameron's stand against bullying:** Cameron went through a really rough time because he was bullied a lot. It made him feel terrible about himself and even affected his grades. But Cameron decided he wasn't going to let the bullies win. He got help, figured out ways to deal with the bullying, and even learned self-defense. His journey wasn't just about stopping the bullies; it was about finding his confidence again. Cameron's story shows that you're way stronger than the mean stuff people say about you.

Lessons from the Stories

Even though these stories are all different, they've got some cool stuff in common about getting stronger and growing. Check it out:

From Jaxon, we see that sticking with it and finding ways to work with our own challenges can make a big difference. It's all about finding what works best for you.

Ava's journey shows us that even when things feel really tough, we can learn to carry our pain and keep going. Going through hard stuff can actually make us understand ourselves better and love others more.

And from Cameron, we learn that reaching out for help and finding ways to feel good about yourself, even when things are tough, is super important. It's about finding your own strength, even when it feels like everything's against you.

Encouraging Empathy

Sharing these stories isn't just about telling cool tales; it's about bringing people together and helping them understand each other better. When you hear about others facing tough times and coming out stronger, it reminds you that you're not alone in your struggles. It builds a bond of caring and understanding among everyone, showing that getting through tough stuff isn't just something you do alone – it's something we all do together.

These stories aren't just about being tough; they're about showing how much we can all grow and become stronger, no matter what life throws our way. They remind us that even when things are hard, there's always a chance to learn and become better versions of ourselves. So, as you keep moving forward, let these stories inspire you to face your own challenges with bravery, knowing that each hurdle is just another step on your journey to becoming the awesome person you're meant to be.

And hey, don't forget to check out the Growth Mindset Experiment waiting for you at the end of this book – it's going to be awesome!

6

SAILING THE DIGITAL WAVES: NAVIGATING SOCIAL MEDIA

"A single act of kindness throws out roots in all directions, and the roots spring up and make new trees." – Amelia Earhart

---

IMAGINE THIS: every like, comment, or share on social media is like a tiny ripple, all coming together to shape the huge ocean of your emotions. In this digital sea, it's easy to feel lost, caught between connecting with others and feeling isolated. Social media is meant to bring us closer, but sometimes it seems like it does the opposite. In this online world, your emotional intelligence is your anchor, helping you handle the ups and downs with mindfulness and strength. We've touched on these ideas before, but now it's time to dive deeper.

The Two Sides of Social Media

Social media is like a double-edged sword. On one side, it connects us to people all over the world, letting us share moments, ideas, and support across distances. It's where movements begin, where learning is endless, and where friendships grow regardless of location.

But on the flip side, you see a different story. Endless scrolling through perfect posts can make us compare ourselves and feel worse about who we are. The nonstop notifications can stress us out, leaving us feeling drained instead of fulfilled.

Spotting Unhealthy Social Media Use

It's important to know when social media is starting to have a negative impact. Watch out for signs like:

- Feeling anxious or depressed after being online
- Ignoring face-to-face relationships or daily tasks
- Feeling jealous or unhappy with your own life after comparing it to others online

If you notice these signs, it's time to rethink your social media habits and make some changes.

Benefits of Mindful Social Media Use

Even with its downsides, social media offers great benefits. It's a space for creativity, a tool for change, and a source of education. The key is to use it mindfully. Think of it like a diet for your mind: consuming a balanced mix of content can boost positivity and growth. Follow accounts that inspire you, teach you, or make you happy. Unfollow or mute those that drain your energy or make you feel bad.

Creating a Balanced Social Media Diet

A balanced social media diet is more than just curating your feed; it's about being intentional with how and when you use social media. Here are some tips to get started:

- **Set specific times for social media use:** Designate certain times of the day for checking social media and stick to them. This helps prevent endless scrolling and keeps your online engagement within healthy limits. Some platforms even let you set time limits for your usage.

- **Engage actively, not passively:** Make your time online meaningful by interacting with content in a way that adds value. Leave thoughtful comments, share articles that moved you, and post about your genuine experiences and learnings. For example, I have a group chat with my closest friends where we share reels or TikToks that make us laugh or teach us something new.
- **Take regular breaks:** Stepping away from social media regularly can help you gain perspective and reconnect with yourself and the world around you. Whether it's for an hour, a day, or a week, these breaks can be incredibly refreshing.

Your emotional intelligence can guide you toward meaningful connections and away from comparison and negativity. With intentionality and mindfulness, you can harness social media as a force for positive growth, ensuring that your online journey enriches, rather than depletes, your emotional well-being. By cultivating a balanced approach to social media, you not only protect your mental health but also open yourself to the vast potential for learning, connection, and joy that these platforms offer.

Managing Your Online Identity with Emotional Intelligence

The Concept of Online Identity

Your online identity is like your digital front porch. It's not just about your photos or tweets; it's a mix of your likes, shares, comments, and the pages you follow. Think of it like choosing an outfit for the first day of school—you want to look good, but you also want to be yourself. Using emotional intelligence to shape your online identity means making choices that reflect who you really are while being aware of the digital trail you're leaving behind.

Emotional Intelligence in Self-Presentation

Emotional intelligence helps you present yourself online in a real and thoughtful way. It's about sharing authentically and considering how your posts might affect others. Here are some tips to keep in mind:

- **Pause before posting:** Before you share a photo or status update, ask yourself why you're posting it. Is it to share something meaningful or just to get likes? If it's the latter, think about whether it really represents who you are.
- **Tone matters:** Emotions can be hard to read online. A joke might come across as sarcasm, and concern might be mistaken for criticism. Consider how your words might be interpreted and, if needed, explain your feelings clearly.
- **Share the journey, not just the highlights:** Being real means showing all parts of life, not just the perfect moments. Sharing your struggles and growth can help build deeper connections and remind others that no one's life is as perfect as it seems on social media.

Strategies for Managing Digital Footprints

Everything you do online, from liking a photo to commenting on a post, adds to your digital footprint. Keeping this footprint in check means making sure your online presence matches who you are and who you want to be. Here are some tips to help manage it:

- **Google yourself regularly:** Search your name to see what others might find. This can help you spot old accounts or posts that no longer represent you.

- **Clean up old posts:** Take some time to go through your social media history. Delete or hide posts that don't reflect who you are now.
- **Be thoughtful about your posts:** Think before you post. Share things that add to your online image in a positive way. Imagine your future self looking back on these posts.
- **Learn about digital rights:** Knowing the rules of social media platforms and understanding your rights can help you make smart choices about what you do online.

Building and managing your online identity with emotional intelligence is a bit like taking care of a garden. It needs regular attention, careful handling, and the realization that what you saw today will influence your digital presence tomorrow. Every post, share, and like isn't just about creating an online identity; it's about shaping a digital legacy that mirrors the many sides of the real you.

Dealing with Cyberbullying: Ways to Cope and Rise Above

On the glowing screens of your devices, a dark shadow lurks – cyberbullying. Unlike traditional bullying that stays at school, cyberbullying can follow you home, invading even your safest spaces.

Understanding Cyberbullying

Cyberbullying involves using electronic communication to bully someone, often by sending intimidating or threatening messages. It's not just about direct threats; spreading rumors, sharing embarrassing photos without permission, or sending hurtful messages all fall under this harmful behavior. The anonymity provided by the digital world can make people act in ways they wouldn't in person, making the impact on the recipient even more distressing.

The effects on teen mental health are significant. Victims of cyberbullying may feel anxious, depressed, and see a big hit to their self-esteem. The constant harassment online can make the digital world feel unwelcoming, leading to withdrawal and loneliness.

Coping Strategies

When dealing with cyberbullying, the principles of emotional intelligence – like self-awareness, self-regulation, empathy, and managing relationships – become crucial tools. Here are some strategies to use these tools effectively:

- **Document and avoid engagement:** Keep records of bullying messages or posts, but don't respond to the bully. Engaging can make things worse, while documenting is important for reporting the behavior.
- **Find comfort in self-awareness:** Remember that the bully's words say more about them than they do about you. Self-awareness helps build resilience, letting you separate your worth from the bully's attempts to hurt you.
- **Practice digital self-care:** Set boundaries for your online life. This might mean taking breaks from social media, using tools to block or report bullies, and creating a positive digital space to reduce exposure to negativity.

Reaching Out for Support

Dealing with cyberbullying aftermath is tough, but you don't have to go through it alone. Knowing when and how to seek help shows courage, not weakness. Here's how to reach out:

- **Trusted adults:** Talk to a parent, teacher, or school counselor you trust about what's going on. They can give advice, emotional support, and help you take further action if needed.
- **Friends and peers:** Sharing your experience with friends can give you emotional support and validation.

They can also join you in standing up against the bullying, providing strength in numbers.

- **Professional help:** Sometimes, cyberbullying's impact goes beyond what friends and family can handle. Therapists or counseling services specialize in helping individuals process their experiences and develop coping strategies.

Building a Positive Online Community

Creating a supportive digital space doesn't just help victims of cyberbullying; it enriches everyone's online experience. Here's how you can contribute to a healthier online world:

- **Spread kindness and respect:** Lead by example in your online interactions. Give compliments, share uplifting content, and offer support to those who need it. Small acts of kindness can make a big difference, setting a tone of empathy and respect.
- **Speak out against bullying:** If you see cyberbullying, don't stay silent. Stand up for the victim and report the bullying to the platform. Showing support can disrupt the bully's power and encourage others to take a stand.
- **Educate and raise awareness:** Spread the word about the impact of cyberbullying and the importance of being empathetic online. Whether it's through school projects, social media campaigns, or community discussions, educating others can inspire action against online harassment.

In the face of cyberbullying, you can use the opportunity to practice and promote emotional intelligence, turning challenges into opportunities for growth and positive change. By using coping strategies, seeking support, and building a supportive online community, you can navigate the digital world with resilience, empathy, and bravery, making it a safer place for everyone.

Digital Detox: Achieving Balance in a Connected World

Your screen serves as both a window to the world and a mirror reflecting your digital self. While being constantly connected can enrich your life, it can also drown out the quiet moments needed for personal growth. Knowing when to step back and recharge away from your device isn't just helpful; it's crucial for your emotional and mental well-being.

The Need for Digital Detox

The signals that it's time to take a break from digital devices and social media aren't always loud and clear. More often, they whisper to you through your increasing reliance on screens for entertainment, your dwindling attention span, or your growing discomfort with real solitude – the kind not interrupted by notifications or quick checks of social media. Other signs include feeling drained after spending time online, difficulty enjoying the present without capturing it for online sharing, and a nagging sense that your digital habits are crowding out more meaningful, offline experiences.

Planning a Digital Detox

Starting a digital detox requires more than just wishing to spend less time on your devices. It begins with setting clear, achievable goals. What do you want to get out of your detox? More time for hobbies? Better connections in person? Once you've set your goals, the next step is to create boundaries. This could mean turning off notifications, setting specific no-phone times during the day, or even taking a break from certain apps. Letting friends and family know about your detox plan can help manage expectations and maybe even inspire others to join you.

- **Set clear goals:** Figure out what you want to achieve with your detox.
- **Create boundaries:** Establish rules to help you stick to your detox plan.
- **Communicate with others:** Inform your social circles about your detox to manage expectations.

Do you want to spice up your downtime during a digital detox? Here are some cool ideas to try out:

- **Read those neglected books:** Remember those novels gathering dust on your shelf? It's time to give them some love.
- **Pick up a new hobby:** Always wanted to try painting, coding, or cooking? Now's your chance to dive in!
- **Chill in nature:** Take a breather outside and soak in the beauty of the natural world. Trust me, it's refreshing.
- **Start journaling:** Pour out your thoughts, dreams, and reflections in a journal. It's like having a personal space for your mind.
- **Get moving:** Whether it's yoga, hiking, or busting a move to your favorite tunes, getting active can help you feel more connected to your body and the world around you.

So, what's your pick?

Reflecting on Digital Consumption

Let's take a moment to think about how much time we spend online and how it affects us. It's not about judging ourselves but being curious. How do we feel after scrolling through social media? Do certain apps make us feel good or bad? Reflecting on these things can help us understand our habits better.

During a digital detox, it's good to ask ourselves:

- Do our online habits match our values?
- Do some online activities make us feel bad about ourselves?

Taking a break from screens gives us time to think, breathe, and reset. It's not about ditching technology altogether but finding a balance. We want to enjoy the good stuff online without forgetting about the real world. This way, we can have a healthier relationship with our devices and live a happier life.

Creating Positive Digital Footprints for the Future

Think of your online presence like leaving footprints in the sand, but these marks stay put. Every post, comment, or share adds to your digital footprint, creating a trail of your online activities. Knowing that these traces stick around is key to managing how you're seen online, both now and later.

Your digital footprint is everything you do online, whether you mean to leave a mark or not. From the pics you post on social media to the comments you make in forums, each thing you do shapes this digital image of you. Even the data websites collect about your browsing habits adds to this picture, showing what you're into and how you behave online.

This matters big time, especially for your future in education and work. Colleges and bosses often check out your online presence. If it's positive, showing off your creativity, leadership, or volunteer work, it can open doors for you. But if there's inappropriate stuff or negativity, it could slam those doors shut.

Want to make sure your online vibe is all positive? Check out these tips:

- **Show off your wins and passions:** Share your achievements, hobbies, and projects online. It's not about bragging, but giving people a glimpse into what makes you tick.

- **Think before you post:** Ask yourself if you'd be cool with anyone seeing what you're about to share, even future bosses or colleges.
- **Spread the good vibes:** When you're online, keep it positive. Be kind, respectful, and understanding in your comments and posts. Let's make the digital world a better place, one positive interaction at a time!

Long-Term Implications

Your online actions today can stick with you for a long time. Think about it: colleges, bosses, and even potential partners might check out your online past. This isn't to freak you out, but to remind you that what you do online matters. Here's how to handle your online self for the long haul:

- **Plan ahead:** Before hitting that post button, think about how you'd feel about it a few years down the line. If it's something that might make you cringe or damage your rep in the future, it's better to skip it.
- **Build a positive online image:** Instead of just avoiding the negative stuff, use social media to show off what makes you awesome. Share your hobbies, skills, and achievements. A positive online presence can really make a difference in opening up opportunities.
- **Keep an eye on your digital trail:** Take a moment every now and then to Google yourself. It gives you a peek into how others see your online self. If you spot anything you're not cool with, you can tweak things to reflect the real you better.

Have you noticed some repetitions in this journey so far? For example, how googling yourself regularly can not only help with your long-term digital footprint, but it can also be found as a simple management tool? Emotional intelligence allows for patterns to support and navigate you on this journey.

As you journey through your digital life, every click, post, and comment adds to the story you're telling about yourself. But with a little thought and effort, you can make sure it's a story you're proud of. By understanding how your digital footprints work, realizing their impact on your future, actively shaping a positive online presence, and regularly tidying up your online trails, you're building a digital legacy to be proud of—one that opens doors instead of closing them.

Your digital footprint isn't just a record; it's a powerful tool that can shape how others see you, create new opportunities, and guide your path in life. By managing it wisely, you're setting yourself up for a future full of promise and potential. So as you move forward, remember to be mindful and intentional about the digital breadcrumbs you leave behind.

Next up, you will find a Digital Detox Challenge curated just for you at the end of this book.

7

THE DIGITAL COMPASS: GUIDING YOUR WAY TO GENUINE FRIENDSHIPS

"The only way to have a friend is to be one." – Ralph Waldo Emerson

PICTURE YOURSELF ENTERING a huge digital city. Think of each app and platform as a different neighborhood. Some are like cozy cafes where you feel at home, while others are like busy markets, crowded with strangers. In this city, friendships happen online, crossing over physical distances. Exciting, huh? But it can also feel overwhelming. How do you figure out which online connections are worth your while? Which ones should you invest more in, and when should you call it quits?

This chapter is your guide to navigating the intricate world of online friendships. It's like mastering the rules of etiquette in this digital city, knowing when to be open and when to be cautious. I'll talk about everything from figuring out if these friendships are worthwhile to setting boundaries that keep you healthy, spotting harmful behaviors, and even knowing when it's time to say goodbye. It's all about finding harmony and making sure your online connections add to your life instead of taking away from it.

Navigating Online Friendships: Knowing When to Hold On and When to Let Go

Assessing Online Friendships

The first step to managing online friendships is figuring out which ones truly benefit you. It's a bit like sorting through your closet, deciding which clothes to keep because they fit well and make you feel great, and which ones to give away because they no longer suit you. Here are some things to consider:

- **Reciprocity:** Does the friendship feel balanced, with both of you giving and receiving, or does it seem one-sided?
- **Shared interests and values:** Do you share common interests or values that deepen your bond beyond just chatting?
- **Support and encouragement:** Does the friendship provide emotional support and encouragement, or does it leave you feeling drained and unsure of yourself?

Maintaining Healthy Boundaries

Setting boundaries in online friendships is like creating a map that outlines your personal space in the digital world. It helps you navigate interactions without losing sight of who you are. Here are some tips for establishing and sticking to these boundaries:

- **Be clear about your limits:** Whether it's about what you're comfortable sharing or how often you want to chat, make sure you clearly communicate your boundaries.

- **Use privacy settings:** Most platforms offer privacy settings that let you control who can see your posts or contact you. Take advantage of these tools to enforce your boundaries.
- **Learn to say no:** It's totally fine to turn down friend requests, group chats, or invitations to games if they don't match your interests or values.

Spotting Toxic Relationships

In the digital world, there are shady corners where negativity or toxicity can creep in. Being able to tell when an online friendship falls into this category is key to protecting your emotional health. Signs of a toxic online friendship include:

- **Constant negativity:** If your interactions consistently leave you feeling down or pessimistic, take note.
- **Manipulation or pressure:** Be cautious of friends who try to manipulate you into sharing personal info or doing things you're not okay with.
- **Disregard for boundaries:** A friend who repeatedly ignores your boundaries isn't showing you respect.

Letting Go Gracefully

Recognizing when it's time to end an online friendship that's no longer healthy is an act of self-care. It's not about cutting ties completely, but about understanding that not every connection is meant to last forever. Here's how to do it with kindness and respect:

- **Communicate your feelings:** If you can, explain why you need to step back from the friendship. Being honest can prevent misunderstandings.

- **Gradually distance yourself:** Sometimes, easing away slowly feels better than a sudden exit. Spend less time interacting with their content or in direct conversations.
- **Focus on positive connections:** Put your energy into friendships that bring out the best in you and offer support.

Online friendships have the potential to be deeply meaningful, providing support, laughter, and connection across vast distances. However, just like any other part of life, they demand mindfulness, intentionality, and occasional courage. By evaluating the worth of these friendships, establishing boundaries, identifying toxic dynamics, and gracefully letting go when needed, you help maintain your digital world as a space of happiness, personal development, and authentic bonds.

Privacy and Safety on Social Media: What You Need to Know

Every click, post, and comment leaves a mark; protecting your privacy and staying safe online is as important as knowing how to navigate busy streets. This section highlights key practices to help safeguard your privacy and ensure your safety, so your digital presence reflects the best of who you are.

The Importance of Privacy Settings

Think of your social media profile like your own diary. Just as you wouldn't want anyone to read your diary without permission, adjusting your privacy settings controls who can see your thoughts, photos, and personal details. Social media platforms provide different settings to manage your privacy, like who can view your posts or tag you in photos. Regularly reviewing and updating these settings is the first step in protecting your online presence. It's like checking the locks on your doors and windows—a simple but vital habit.

· · ·

Best Practices for Staying Safe Online

To navigate online communities and friendships safely, follow these guidelines:

- **Think before you share:** Take a moment to think about what you're sharing—whether it's personal info, photos, or locations. Not everything needs to be online. Before posting, ask yourself if you'd be okay with everyone seeing it, especially strangers. If not, consider keeping it offline or sharing it privately.
- **Verify friend requests:** Only accept friend requests from people you know in real life. It's easy for someone to pretend to be someone else online.
- **Be cautious with links and downloads:** Malicious software can hide in innocent-looking links or files. If something seems fishy, it probably is. Avoid clicking on links from unknown sources.
- **Use strong, unique passwords:** Keep your accounts safe with strong passwords, and avoid using the same password for multiple sites. Consider using a password manager to help keep track of them.
- **Regularly check your privacy settings:** Social media platforms often update their privacy policies and settings. Make it a habit to review these settings regularly to ensure they still meet your privacy needs.
- **Control your audience:** Many social media platforms offer features to control who can see your posts. Use these features to make sure your content is only visible to the people you want to see it.

Educational Resources

Staying informed is crucial for navigating the complexities of online privacy and safety. There are many resources available to offer insights and tips to help you protect yourself online. Here are a few to get you started:

- **StaySafeOnline (staysafeonline.org):** Provides a wealth of resources on staying safe online, covering topics from social media safety to cyberbullying prevention.
- **Common Sense Media (commonsensemedia.org):** Offers guides and articles on digital citizenship, internet safety, and managing online privacy.
- **Cyberbully Help (cyberbullyhelp.com):** A resource for understanding and combating cyberbullying, with tools for teens, parents, and educators.
- **ConnectSafely (connectsafely.org):** A nonprofit dedicated to educating users about safety, privacy, and security in the digital world.

Ultimately, the digital world is much like the real one—it offers vast opportunities for connection, learning, and growth. But just as you take precautions in your physical life, you must do so online. By setting privacy controls, practicing safe online behavior, managing your digital footprint, and continually seeking knowledge, you ensure that your journey through the digital city is not only safe but also enriching and enjoyable.

The Impact of Comparisons: Overcoming Social Media Envy

Feeling down when you're checking out your social media? You're not alone. It's super common to feel a bit bummed when you see all the cool stuff people post. Your chill Friday night might seem kinda blah compared to their exciting adventures, and suddenly, your achievements don't feel as awesome. That's what we call social media envy. It's that mix of feelings when you see other people's lives looking super cool while yours feels just okay. And hey, it's totally normal, even though not many folks talk about it openly.

Understanding Social Media Envy

Social media envy happens because we naturally compare ourselves to others. It's important to realize that feeling this way isn't a bad thing—it's just how our brains work when we see all those polished versions of people's lives online. Once you recognize it, you're on the right track to dealing with it and not letting it bring you down.

Reality vs. Presentation

It's all about knowing the gap between what's real and what's shown. Think of social media as a stage where everyone puts up their best performances. Those posts are real, but they're carefully chosen and sometimes exaggerated. They don't show the everyday stuff, the tough times, or the unfiltered reality we all deal with. Remembering this helps you see through the glam and realize we're all just human, facing similar ups and downs.

Strategies to Counteract Envy

When envy sneaks in while you're scrolling, these tricks can help you get back to feeling good:

- **Switch it up:** When you start feeling jealous, try focusing on the things in your life that make you happy. Maybe it's a hobby you enjoy or spending time with your pals and family.
- **Filter your feed:** If certain accounts make you feel bad about yourself, consider unfollowing them. Follow pages that make you feel inspired instead of ones that make you compare yourself.
- **Say thanks:** Practicing gratitude can really help fight envy. Take a moment each day to think about the things

you're grateful for. It shifts your focus from what you don't have to what you do.

- **Get real:** Spending time with friends and family offline can remind you that there's more to life than what's on your screen. Face-to-face hangouts show you the depth and realness of life beyond the internet.

Focusing on Personal Growth

The best way to beat social media envy is to focus on your own growth instead of comparing yourself to others. Here's how to do it:

- **Set your own goals:** Figure out what success and happiness mean to you. Set goals based on your own standards, and celebrate your progress toward them.
- **Embrace your journey:** Remember, everyone's journey is different with its own ups and downs. Trust that you're on the right path for you.
- **Seek inspiration, not comparison:** Use others' achievements to inspire you, not intimidate you. Let their successes motivate you to chase your own dreams.
- **Invest in self-discovery:** Spend time learning about yourself—your strengths, passions, and values. The better you know yourself, the less you'll feel the need to compare your life to others.

Remember, your worth isn't measured by likes, comments, or the perfect photos you see online. It's found in the real moments you experience, the personal growth you pursue, and the genuine connections you make. By recognizing and dealing with social media envy, you can enjoy these platforms for what they truly offer—a way to share, connect, and inspire—while staying grounded in the reality of your own valuable, unfiltered life.

Authenticity Online: Being True to Yourself in a Digital World

Every post, like, and share creates a picture of who you are. Staying true to yourself is more than just a good idea—it's essential for real connections and genuine self-expression. In a world of curated feeds and highlight reels, being authentic is like a breath of fresh air, a reminder of what's real in a sea of filters and fake moments.

The Value of Authenticity

Why does being authentic matter, especially online? Authenticity bridges your inner world with the digital one, allowing you to share your true thoughts, feelings, and beliefs. This honesty not only creates deeper connections with others who appreciate the real you but also boosts your self-esteem. Each time you choose to be authentic, you affirm your worth and celebrate your individuality.

- **Cultivates genuine connections:** Authentic interactions attract people who value the real you, forming the foundation for meaningful online friendships.
- **Enhances self-esteem:** Every authentic post serves as a reminder of your values and integrity, reinforcing self-respect and confidence.
- **Encourages others:** Your authenticity can inspire others to shed their digital disguises, fostering a culture of honesty and openness.

Challenges to Authenticity

Staying true to yourself online isn't always easy. The lure of likes and the pressure to show an idealized self can be strong. Social media algorithms often favor content that's glamorous and happy, leaving little room for the real, messy parts of life.

- **The like economy:** Chasing validation through likes can lead to a polished persona that follows popular trends instead of reflecting your true interests.
- **Fear of judgment:** Worrying about negative feedback can stop you from sharing opinions or parts of your life that are different from the norm.
- **Comparison trap:** Seeing others' seemingly perfect lives can hurt your confidence, making you want to hide or change parts of your true self.

Expressing Your True Self

How can you overcome these challenges and stay true to yourself online? It begins with small acts of courage and realizing that your worth isn't tied to online approval.

- **Share your passions:** Post about activities, causes, or topics you genuinely care about, even if they're not popular.
- **Embrace imperfection:** Let go of the need to be perfect. Share real moments and feelings—your struggles, not just your successes.
- **Set your standards:** Define what authenticity means to you and stick to these standards instead of seeking external validation.

The Role of Emotional Intelligence

Emotional intelligence helps you stay true to yourself online. It makes you aware when you're not being genuine and gives you the strength to stick to your values, even when it's tough.

- **Self-awareness:** Knowing your values, interests, and principles helps you create posts that reflect who you really are, not just what you think others want to see.

- **Self-regulation:** Emotional intelligence helps you resist the urge to fit in or seek validation. It encourages you to post things that are true to you.
- **Empathy:** Understanding and valuing the authenticity in others can strengthen your own commitment to being real, creating a ripple effect of sincerity in your online circles.

In a digital world where things can be easily faked, being authentic is a powerful act of self-love and honesty. It's about showing up as you are, embracing all parts of yourself. This not only improves your online interactions but also reinforces your true identity, making sure the person behind the screen is the same as the one you show to the world.

Supporting Peers Online: Building a Positive Digital Community

Every interaction online can create a ripple effect, so the support you offer your peers can truly make a difference. Just as a single kind word can brighten someone's day, your digital gestures of support can light up the darker corners of the internet, creating spaces that are not only safe but also nurturing and positive.

The Power of Support

It's easy to feel lost or overlooked online. Yet, when you reach out with a word of encouragement or a gesture of support, you throw a lifeline to those who might be struggling in silence. This act of kindness doesn't just lift them; it elevates you too, strengthening the bonds of your digital community and reminding you of the power of unity and empathy.

Ways to Support Friends Online

There are tons of ways to support your friends online, from simple actions to more involved efforts. Here are a few ideas to get you started:

- **Leaving positive comments:** A nice comment on someone's post can totally make their day. Whether you're congratulating them on something cool they did or offering comfort when they're down, your words can be a real boost.
- **Sharing resources:** If you find a helpful article, video, or post, share it with someone who might find it useful. It's like saying, "Hey, I thought of you when I saw this!"
- **Creating encouragement groups:** Platforms like Facebook and Discord let you create groups focused on shared interests or support. Starting or joining these groups provides a space for positive conversations and shared experiences.

Creating Positive Spaces

Building positive online spaces takes patience, care, and a willingness to block out negativity. Here's how you can help:

- **Model respectful behavior:** Set an example with your interactions. Be open and respectful, even if you disagree with someone.
- **Report and stand against negativity:** If you see bullying or harassment, don't engage with it—report it. Standing up against negativity helps keep your digital space safe.
- **Encourage inclusivity:** Make everyone feel welcome. Celebrate diversity and encourage people who might be shy to speak up. A positive space is one where everyone feels seen and heard.

Being a Good Digital Citizen

Being a good digital citizen means recognizing your responsibility to make online communities better. It involves:

- **Understanding the impact of your words:** Remember that behind every profile is a real person. Your words can affect them deeply, so always choose kindness and empathy.
- **Educating yourself and others:** Stay informed about issues like cyberbullying and privacy concerns. Share this knowledge to help create a safer, more informed community.
- **Promoting a culture of respect and empathy:** Support respect and empathy everywhere online. Whether it's in the comments of a YouTube video or a heated Twitter thread, your voice can guide the conversation toward understanding and compassion.

As you wrap up this journey into supporting peers online and creating positive spaces, remember how powerful your digital interactions can be. From the gentle power of a kind comment to the collective strength of a community united in kindness, your actions online help build a digital world that's not only safe but also enriching.

Carry these lessons with you, applying them not just online but in all areas of your life. As you move forward, you'll build on these foundations, learning to navigate the complexities of digital well-being, making your journey as rewarding and fulfilling as possible.

And, of course, you will find a Digital Kindness Experiment curated just for you at the end of this book.

8

ANCHORING IN SELF-CARE: THE FOUNDATION OF EMOTIONAL WELL-BEING

"Nourishing yourself in a way that helps you blossom in the direction you want to go is attainable, and you are worth the effort." — Deborah Day

PICTURE YOUR MIND as a city during the peak hours of the day. Thoughts zoom by like cars on a freeway, emotions rise and dip like the city's skyline, and amidst all this chaos, you're trying to navigate through, hoping not to crash. Now, imagine if this city had a serene park right in its center, a place you could retreat to, find your calm, and just breathe. That's what self-care does for your emotional intelligence; it's your mind's oasis, vital for maintaining balance and clarity amidst life's hustles.

Self-care often gets tossed into the "luxury" basket, something you'll get around to "someday." But let's set the record straight: it's not a luxury; it's essential maintenance for your inner world, as critical as oil changes are for your car. Ignoring it doesn't just wear you down; it makes every emotional bump feel harder, every decision more complex.

Integrating Self-Care

Self-care is about more than bubble baths and spa days. It's about creating moments in your day that remind you, you matter. When you're feeling good—physically, mentally, emotionally—you're more tuned in to your emotions and better equipped to handle whatever life tosses your way. It's like putting on your oxygen mask first; you're securing your well-being so you can be present and supportive in your interactions with others.

Self-Care as Emotional Regulation

Let's break down how self-care plays a role in managing your varying emotions. Think about the last time you were really hungry—everything felt more intense, right? That's because not taking care of your basic needs directly impacts your emotional state. Regular self-care acts buffer you from the edge, making it easier to identify your emotions without being overwhelmed by them. It's your emotional shock absorber, softening the highs and lows so you can navigate your feelings with more grace.

Self-Compassion

At the heart of self-care lies self-compassion. It's treating yourself with the same kindness and understanding you'd offer a good friend. This doesn't mean letting yourself off the hook for everything, but acknowledging that being too hard on yourself serves no one. When you mess up—and you will because you're human—self-compassion allows you to acknowledge the slip-up without letting it define you.

Holistic Approach to Self-Care

True self-care touches every part of your being. Here's how to ensure you're covering all bases:

- **Physical:** This is the stuff you often think of: eating nourishing foods, getting enough sleep, staying active. It's about respecting your body's needs and recognizing its direct link to your emotional well-being.
- **Emotional:** Carve out time for activities that refill your emotional cup. This could mean journaling, therapy sessions, or heart-to-hearts with friends. It's anything that helps you process and express your feelings constructively.
- **Mental:** Keep your brain engaged and inspired. Learn something new, dive into a book, or solve puzzles. Challenge your mind in a way that feels refreshing, not draining.
- **Social:** Connect with people who lift you up. It's easy to feel isolated, so making time for meaningful connections is crucial.
- **Spiritual:** This looks different for everyone. It might be meditation, spending time in nature, or engaging in a religious community. It's about connecting with something larger than yourself, whatever that means to you.

Mindfulness Practices for Daily Life

Imagine your mind like a sky, sometimes clear, sometimes filled with passing clouds. Thoughts and emotions can cloud that sky, but mindfulness is the gentle breeze that clears it, allowing you to see the blue sky once again. Mindfulness, at its core, is about being fully present, engaging with the here and now, and accepting your thoughts and feelings without judgment. It's a skill that, when woven into the fabric of your daily life, can significantly amplify your emotional intelligence, providing clarity and calm in the emotional storms that sometimes hit.

Let's explore.

· · ·

Basics of Mindfulness

Mindfulness is the practice of anchoring your attention to the present moment, observing your thoughts, feelings, bodily sensations, and the environment around you with a curious, non-judgmental stance. It's about noticing the details of your life as it unfolds, rather than living on autopilot. This heightened awareness can transform your relationship with your emotions, turning reactive impulses into thoughtful responses. It's a tool that, once mastered, can offer a profound sense of peace and centeredness amidst life's chaos.

Simple Mindfulness Exercises

Incorporating mindfulness into your routine doesn't have to be a grand event; it can be as simple as pausing for a few moments to breathe. Here are some practices to get you started, which, after reading the previous chapters, may sound familiar:

- **Mindful breathing:** Spend a few minutes each day sitting quietly, focusing on your breath. Notice the sensation of air entering and leaving your nostrils, the rise and fall of your chest, the rhythm of your breathing. When your mind wanders, gently bring your focus back to your breath.
- **Sensory observation:** Choose an everyday activity like eating a meal or taking a shower. Focus on the sensory experiences involved—the taste of the food, the warmth of the water, the scent of soap. Engage fully with the moment, using your senses as anchors to the present.
- **Mindful walking:** Take a short walk, paying attention to the sensation of your feet touching the ground, the sounds around you, the temperature of the air, and the sights you pass. Walk as if you're experiencing everything for the first time.

Mindfulness and Emotional Awareness

Practicing mindfulness cultivates a deep, intimate understanding of your emotional landscape. By observing your thoughts and feelings without getting caught up in them, you learn to recognize your emotional triggers and patterns. This awareness creates space between stimulus and response, giving you the power to choose how you react. It's like watching clouds drift across the sky—you see them, acknowledge them, but don't get swept away by them. This space is where wisdom resides, allowing you to navigate your emotions with insight and grace.

Incorporating Mindfulness into School and Social Activities

Mindfulness isn't just for quiet, solitary moments; it can enrich every aspect of your life, including your school and social activities. Here's how to bring mindfulness into these areas:

- **In class:** Before a test or during a challenging lesson, take a moment to focus on your breath, grounding yourself in the present. This can help calm nerves and enhance concentration. Listen actively during lectures, fully engaging with the material rather than letting your mind wander to what's for lunch.
- **With friends:** Be fully present in conversations, listening with your whole being rather than planning what you'll say next. Notice your reactions and emotions as you interact, approaching each moment with curiosity and openness.
- **During extracurriculars:** Whether you're on the sports field or in the art room, use this time as an opportunity to immerse yourself in the present. Pay attention to the physical sensations, the joy of participation, and the companionship with teammates or peers.

Mindfulness is a gentle yet powerful tool that can transform your relationship with yourself and the world around you. By integrating mindful practices into your daily life, you cultivate a heightened sense of emotional awareness and a deeper connection to the present moment. This connection, in turn, enriches your experiences, allowing you to engage with life fully and navigate its ups and downs with a steady, calm mind.

The Importance of Sleep: Resting Your Mind and Emotions

Sleep's role extends far beyond mere physical rest. It is a crucial component in the construction and maintenance of emotional resilience and mental clarity.

Sleep and Emotional Processing

Each night, as you drift into sleep, your brain embarks on a meticulous process of sifting through the day's emotional experiences. This nocturnal journey allows you to process complex emotions and consolidate memories, essentially "cleaning up" your mental workspace. Without adequate sleep, this process is hindered, leading to increased sensitivity to emotional stimuli and a diminished capacity to manage stress and anxiety. It's as if sleep puts the day's emotional chaos into perspective, enabling you to start the next day with a clearer, more balanced outlook.

Creating a Sleep-Positive Environment

Crafting an environment that whispers, "It's time to rest," can significantly enhance the quality of your sleep. Consider these suggestions to transform your bedroom into a sleep sanctuary:

- **Soothing colors:** Opt for calming hues in your bedroom décor. Soft blues, greens, and lavenders can have a tranquil effect on your mind, promoting relaxation.

- **Comfort is key:** Invest in a comfortable mattress and pillows. The physical aspect of where you sleep plays a significant role in how well you rest.
- **Controlled lighting:** Dim lights signal to your brain that it's time to wind down. Consider blackout curtains or an eye mask if you're sensitive to light.
- **A clutter-free space:** A tidy room can lead to a more peaceful mind. Try to keep your sleeping area free from clutter and distractions.

Dealing with Sleep Challenges

For many teens, challenges like insomnia or irregular sleep patterns are all too common, yet there are strategies to navigate these hurdles:

- **Consistent sleep schedule:** Try to go to bed and wake up at the same time each day. Regularity reinforces your body's sleep-wake cycle, making it easier to fall asleep.
- **Wind-down routine:** Establish a calming pre-sleep ritual. This could involve reading, gentle stretching, or listening to soft music. The key is to signal to your body that it's time to slow down.
- **Limit naps:** While tempting, long naps can disrupt your nighttime sleep. If you need to nap, aim for short power naps of 20-30 minutes earlier in the day.
- **Seek professional advice:** If sleep issues persist, it might be time to consult a healthcare provider. Sometimes, underlying issues need to be addressed to restore healthy sleep patterns.

Sleep Hygiene

Good sleep hygiene encompasses a set of practices and habits that are conducive to sleeping well on a regular basis. Here are foundational elements to incorporate into your routine:

- **Screen time limitations:** The blue light emitted by screens can interfere with your ability to fall asleep. Aim to put away electronic devices at least an hour before bedtime.
- **Physical activity:** Regular exercise can improve the quality and duration of your sleep. However, try to avoid vigorous workouts close to bedtime as they might keep you awake.
- **Mind your caffeine intake:** Caffeine is a stimulant that can stay in your system for hours, making it harder to fall asleep. Try to avoid caffeine late in the day.
- **Create a sleep-inviting atmosphere:** Make your bedroom a place for sleep only. Keep it cool, dark, and quiet. Consider using white noise machines or earplugs if you're easily disturbed by outside noise.

By prioritizing sleep and making it a non-negotiable part of your daily routine, you're not just investing in better rest; you're building your emotional resilience, sharpening your mental clarity, and enhancing your overall quality of life. Sleep isn't just a pause from your busy life; it's an active and powerful tool in your emotional and mental health toolkit, one that deserves your respect and attention.

Nutrition and Emotional Well-Being: Feeding Your Mind and Body

You've likely heard the phrase "You are what you eat," but have you ever stopped to consider how deeply the food you consume influences not just your physical health but your emotions and mental state as well? It turns out, the connection between diet and mood is more significant than many realize, acting as a continuous feedback loop that can either uplift or dampen your emotional well-being.

. . .

The Connection Between Diet and Mood

Imagine your brain as a high-performance vehicle. Just like a car needs quality fuel to run smoothly, your brain requires the right nutrients to function at its best. When your diet is rich in essential vitamins, minerals, and antioxidants, it's like giving your brain premium fuel that enhances mood regulation, cognitive function, and overall mental health. On the other hand, a diet high in processed foods, sugar, and unhealthy fats can act like contaminated fuel, potentially leading to or exacerbating feelings of anxiety, depression, and lethargy.

Foods That Boost Emotional Health

So, what constitutes premium fuel for your brain? Here's a rundown of mood-boosting foods that can help keep your emotional engine running smoothly:

- **Omega-3 fatty acids:** Found in fatty fish like salmon, walnuts, and flaxseeds, omega-3s play a crucial role in brain health, helping to improve mood and combat depression.
- **Whole grains:** Foods like oatmeal, quinoa, and brown rice are rich in tryptophan, an amino acid that helps produce serotonin, the "feel-good" neurotransmitter.
- **Leafy greens:** Spinach, kale, and other greens are packed with folate, a vitamin that contributes to the production of dopamine and serotonin.
- **Berries:** Blueberries, strawberries, and other berries contain antioxidants that help reduce inflammation and stress.
- **Nuts and seeds:** Almonds, chia seeds, and pumpkin seeds are great sources of magnesium, a mineral that can help with stress management and sleep.

Incorporating a variety of these foods into your meals can create a solid foundation for emotional stability and mental clarity.

Mindful Eating Practices

Mindful eating invites you to fully experience and savor your food, turning mealtime into a moment of reflection and appreciation. This practice encourages you to tune into your body's hunger and fullness cues, leading to a healthier relationship with food and emotions. Here's how to get started:

- **Eat without distractions:** Sit down for meals without the TV on or phone in hand. This allows you to fully focus on the experience of eating.
- **Slow down:** Take your time with each bite, chewing slowly to savor the flavors and textures. This helps improve digestion and satisfaction with meals.
- **Check-in with your emotions:** Before eating, ask yourself if you're truly hungry or if you're reaching for food in response to stress, boredom, or other emotions. Each time I want to eat, I ask myself, "Am I hungry, thirsty, bored, or tired?" This helps me gauge what my body actually needs. Learning to discern different cues can prevent emotional eating.

Developing Healthy Eating Habits

For many teens, balancing school, social life, and extracurriculars can make healthy eating feel like a challenge. However, with a few strategies, nourishing your body and mind can seamlessly fit into your busy schedule:

- **Plan ahead:** Spend a bit of time each week planning your meals. This can help ensure you have healthy options on hand when hunger strikes, preventing the temptation to reach for less nutritious snacks.

- **Stay hydrated:** Sometimes, thirst disguises as hunger. Keeping a water bottle handy and sipping throughout the day can keep you hydrated and help regulate your appetite.
- **Listen to your body:** Pay attention to how different foods make you feel. You might notice that some foods leave you feeling energized and focused, while others make you feel sluggish or irritable. Use this feedback to guide your food choices.
- **Make it a family affair:** Involve your family in meal planning and preparation. Cooking together can be a fun way to explore new foods and share the responsibility of making healthy meals.

The relationship between nutrition and emotional well-being underscores the profound impact your dietary choices have on your mental and emotional landscapes. By treating food as nourishment for both body and mind, you equip yourself with yet another tool in your emotional intelligence toolkit, fostering resilience, clarity, and a sense of well-being that radiates from the inside out. Remember, the journey to emotional balance begins on your plate, one mindful bite at a time.

Creative Outlets for Emotional Expression: Writing, Art, and Music

Creativity acts as a mirror to your deepest self, offering a canvas to color your emotions in hues unseen and melodies unheard. The act of creating—be it through words, strokes, or notes—opens doors to understanding your emotional worlds in ways words alone cannot capture. This section explores the heart of using creativity as a conduit for emotional expression, and the profound impact it can have on your inner self.

Expressive Arts as Emotional Outlets

The path to emotional intelligence is rich with the language of art, music, and writing. These forms of expression offer a sanctuary for emotions, providing a safe space to explore and articulate feelings that might otherwise remain hidden. The act of painting, for instance, can translate complex emotions into a visual language, offering insights into your internal states. Similarly, music can resonate with your feelings, providing comfort and understanding, while writing allows you to untangle and examine your emotional threads in detail.

- **Art** serves as a visual diary, capturing emotions in color and form.
- **Music** echoes your feelings, creating a resonance that can soothe or energize.
- **Writing** offers a narrative to your emotional journey, helping you make sense of your experiences.

Starting a Creative Practice

Embarking on a creative journey requires no prerequisites; you need not identify as an artist, musician, or writer to explore these realms. The key lies in allowing yourself the freedom to express without judgment. Here are some tips to foster your creative practice:

- **Set aside time:** Dedicate a few minutes each day to your chosen form of expression. It does not need to be lengthy; even brief periods of creativity can have a significant impact.
- **Create without expectations:** Let go of the notion of "good" or "bad" art. The value lies in the process, not the product.

- **Gather simple materials:** Start with what you have. A pencil and paper for writing or drawing, or even free music apps for composing, can set the stage for creativity.

Sharing Creativity for Connection

Sharing your creative work can be a powerful way to connect with others on an emotional level. It offers a glimpse into your inner world, fostering deeper understanding and empathy. Consider these avenues for sharing:

- **Social media platforms:** Use these spaces to share your creations and engage with a community of like-minded individuals.
- **Personal blogs or websites:** Create a dedicated space to curate and showcase your work.
- **Local community groups:** Join art, writing, or music groups where you can share and receive feedback in a supportive environment.

Creative Activities and Mindfulness

The act of creating brings you into the present moment, anchoring you in a state of flow where time seems to stand still. This focus on the present is a form of mindfulness that can quiet the mind and ease emotional turmoil. The repetitive motion of brush strokes, the rhythm of typing, or the melody of a song can serve as meditative practices that center and calm the mind.

- **Drawing or painting:** Focus on each stroke, observing the colors as they blend, and notice the feelings that arise.
- **Playing an instrument:** Pay attention to the sensation of the instrument in your hands, the sound of the notes, and the emotions they evoke.

- **Creative writing:** Immerse yourself in the storytelling, feeling the words as they flow from your thoughts onto the page.

In these moments of creative immersion, you're not just making art; you're engaging in an act of mindfulness that brings clarity and peace to your emotional world. It's a practice that, over time, can enhance your emotional intelligence, providing you with tools to navigate your emotions with creativity and insight.

Keep note that in the exploration of creative outlets for emotional expression, it's clear that engaging in writing, art, and music offers a profound way to understand and articulate your emotional land-scape. These practices not only enrich your life with beauty and creativity but also strengthen your emotional intelligence, offering pathways to explore and express your feelings in meaningful, healing ways. They remind you that the journey to understanding your emotions can be as colorful, nuanced, and profound as the art you create. So, as you move forward, take the lessons learned with you from your creative endeavors, allowing them to illuminate your path to emotional growth and resilience.

You already know what's coming at this point, but a 21-Day Emotional Wellness Journey Challenge was curated just for you at the end of this book!

9

LEARNING THE MAP OF YOU: EMOTIONAL INTELLIGENCE AS A JOURNEY

"The discipline of writing something down is the first step toward making it happen." — Lee Iacocca

IMAGINE THIS: Your emotions are like a palette of paints, each color bright and full of possibilities. Sometimes, the colors mix perfectly, creating beautiful and clear moments in your life. Other times, they can get messy and blur the picture of how you feel. In those messy moments, journaling isn't just writing in a notebook; it becomes a powerful way to understand and navigate your feelings.

Benefits of Journaling for Emotional Intelligence

Journaling works wonders for your mind and soul. It's like having a conversation with yourself, where you're both the speaker and the listener. This self-talk can reveal why you feel the way you do by uncovering your emotional triggers and patterns. It's like piecing together a puzzle, with each journal entry helping to form a clearer picture of your emotional self.

- **Aids in emotional self-awareness:** Writing down your thoughts and feelings regularly sharpens your ability to recognize and name your emotions, which is a key part of emotional intelligence.
- **Enhances emotional regulation:** Journaling about tough experiences helps you process and manage intense emotions, giving you a healthy way to express them.
- **Boosts problem-solving abilities:** By putting your thoughts on paper, you might find solutions to problems that weren't clear in the chaos of your mind.

Journaling Techniques and Prompts

Starting a journal can feel overwhelming, making you unsure of where to begin. Here are some techniques and prompts to help you get started:

- **Stream of consciousness:** Just let it flow. Write whatever comes to mind without worrying about coherence or punctuation. This technique can uncover thoughts and feelings you weren't aware of.
- **Emotion-focused entries:** Choose an emotion you felt strongly during the day and explore it in depth. What triggered it? How did you react? Could you have responded differently?
- **Gratitude journaling:** End each day by listing three things you're grateful for. This practice can shift your focus from what's lacking to what's abundant in your life.

Reflective Journaling

Reflection is the core of journaling. It's more than just noting down events—it's about exploring why they matter and what they reveal about you. After you write, take a moment to review your entry and ask yourself:

- What did I learn about myself?
- How can I use this understanding in the future?
- Is there a pattern in my thoughts or behaviors that I want to change?

This practice can be eye-opening, giving you insights into your growth areas and highlighting your strengths.

Privacy and Personal Space

Your journal is your sanctuary, a private space where you can be completely honest. Keeping it private lets you be as open as you need to be without worrying about judgment. Here are some tips to keep your journal safe:

- **Find a safe spot:** Keep your journal in a place where others are unlikely to find it.
- **Digital journals:** If you prefer typing, use secure journaling apps that require a password or fingerprint to access.
- **Set boundaries:** If you're worried about someone reading your journal, explain to them how important your privacy is for your emotional well-being.

Journaling is a journey into yourself, helping you navigate your emotions with more clarity and understanding. Over time, it can change not just how you see yourself but also how you interact with the world. By journaling regularly, you're not just recording your life; you're exploring your emotions and learning more about who you are.

The Power of Gratitude: Shifting Your Emotional Perspective

Gratitude isn't just about saying "thank you." It's about recognizing and appreciating the good things around you. This practice can change your mental and emotional state. By focusing on what you have instead of what's missing, you'll see a shift in how you view the world and your place in it. This change is real—studies show that practicing gratitude regularly can reduce stress, improve sleep, and increase overall happiness.

Understanding Gratitude

Gratitude is about recognizing the good in life, even on tough days. It's seeing the light in dark times and realizing that challenges can teach valuable lessons. This understanding opens your heart, making you feel more connected to yourself and the world around you. The beauty of gratitude is in its simplicity and its powerful ability to brighten your emotional landscape.

Gratitude Practices

Making gratitude a habit can be easy and enjoyable, fitting right into your daily routine. Here are some practices to try:

- **Gratitude journals:** Spend a few minutes each evening writing down three things you're grateful for. They can be as big as a life-changing event or as small as the warmth of the sun on your face.
- **Gratitude meditation:** Start or end your day with a short meditation focused on gratitude. Visualize the people, moments, or experiences you're thankful for, and feel the warmth of gratitude with each breath.
- **Gratitude jar:** Fill a jar with notes about moments or things you're grateful for. Watching the jar fill up can be a powerful visual reminder of the abundance in your life.
- **Thank-you notes:** Write thank-you notes, not just for gifts or big gestures, but for everyday kindnesses that often go unnoticed. This practice spreads joy and strengthens your own feelings of gratitude.

Gratitude and Resilience

When you face challenges, it's easy to get stuck in negative thoughts. Gratitude, however, helps you build resilience by finding the silver lining in tough situations. It doesn't make the difficulty go away, but it gives you the strength and hope to face it. Over time, this mindset helps you bounce back from life's storms with more agility and optimism.

The Ripple Effect of Gratitude

Gratitude has a contagious nature, reaching far beyond the person who practices it. When you express gratitude, it not only lifts your own spirits but also has a big impact on those around you. It creates a cycle of kindness and appreciation, making relationships stronger and fostering a positive atmosphere where support and connections thrive. Here are some ways gratitude can spread through your interactions:

- **Positive reinforcement:** When you genuinely appreciate someone's efforts or kindness, it encourages them to keep being kind, not just to you but to others, too.
- **Shared joy:** Sharing what you're grateful for can inspire others to think about their own blessings, making everyone feel happier.
- **Deepened connections:** Expressing gratitude can strengthen relationships, building a foundation of respect and appreciation.
- **Collective resilience:** A community that practices gratitude supports each other during tough times, making it easier to face challenges together.

Gratitude may seem simple, but it sheds light on the complexities of your emotions. It shows you that even in the midst of different feelings, there's always something to be thankful for. It teaches you to find joy in the little things and to see the value in every moment, no matter how small. Gratitude becomes more than just a habit—it becomes a way of life, subtly changing how you interact with the world and with yourself, lighting up your path with a gentle, lasting glow.

Learning from Role Models: How Mentors Can Shape Your Emotional Landscape

Your role models and mentors offer priceless insights that can guide you through the ups and downs of your emotions and daily choices. Their stories and advice not only deepen your understanding but also give you hope and show you what's possible.

Role Models and Emotional Growth

The influence of a mentor or role model in your emotional development can hardly be overstated. Imagine a lighthouse guiding ships through foggy nights; similarly, role models illuminate the way, showing you how to handle emotions with grace, make decisions with confidence, and navigate challenges with resilience. They are living examples of emotional intelligence in action, demonstrating how to engage with our feelings, understand others, and build relationships rooted in empathy and respect.

Finding Role Models

Finding a mentor or role model might seem like a big task, but they're often closer than you realize. They could be a teacher who listens to you, a calm family member, or a community leader who inspires you. Here's how to start finding and connecting with potential role models:

- **Reflect on qualities you admire:** Think about the traits or accomplishments you admire and want to develop. This can help you spot people who have those qualities.
- **Reach out:** Don't be afraid to tell someone you admire them and ask for advice or help. Most people are happy to share what they know.
- **Engage in communities:** Join clubs, groups, or online forums that match your interests. You might find mentors there who are passionate about the same things you are.

Learning from their Experiences

Once you've connected with a mentor or role model, it's time to start learning. Be curious and ask them about their journey— the challenges they faced, how they tackled them, and the lessons they learned. Their experiences can offer you practical advice and emotional strategies that you can apply to your own life. Remember, the goal isn't to copy their path but to gather insights that can help you navigate your own emotional journey more effectively.

- **Active listening:** Listen carefully when they share their stories or advice. There's a lot to learn from both their successes and failures.
- **Ask thoughtful questions:** Don't hesitate to ask about how they handle specific emotional challenges or make tough decisions. This can reveal strategies that you can use in your own life.
- **Reflect on their advice:** After your conversations, take some time to think about what they've shared. How does it relate to your own life and emotional goals?

Being a Role Model

As you grow and learn, you'll eventually have the opportunity to guide others, becoming the mentor you once looked for. This shift is a natural part of the learning process, allowing you to give back and help someone else grow emotionally.

- **Live your values:** Be aware of how you handle your emotions and relationships. Your actions can inspire others, even without you intending to mentor them directly.
- **Be open to sharing:** Whether it's a sibling, a friend, or someone in your community, be willing to share your experiences and the lessons you've learned. Your journey, with its highs and lows, can offer hope and guidance to others.
- **Emphasize empathy, integrity, and emotional intelligence:** Model the importance of understanding and managing emotions, both yours and others. Show how empathy and integrity create strong, meaningful connections.

Role models and mentors have a big impact. They not only guide you through your emotions and decisions but also remind you of the power of empathy, integrity, and emotional intelligence. By following their example, you learn to navigate your own emotional journey better. And eventually, you'll become a guide for others who are on a similar path.

Planning Your Personal Growth Path: Next Steps in Emotional Intelligence

As you journey through emotional intelligence, you've collected tools, insights, and practices that shed light on different aspects of your inner world. Now, as you stand at a crossroads, armed with knowledge, it's time to widen your path forward. This next phase involves integrating your learning into your everyday life, turning insights into actions, and aspirations into accomplishments.

Setting Personal Growth Goals

Imagine your future self – what aspects of emotional intelligence do you see shining brightly? Is it your resilience in tough times, or maybe your empathy touching the lives of those around you? Setting goals is like drawing a map for this journey, marking the destinations you want to explore within yourself.

- **Be specific:** Instead of a broad goal like "I want to be more empathetic," focus on specific situations where you want to apply empathy. For instance, "I'll practice active listening with my friends when they share their problems."
- **Achievable milestones:** Break your goals into smaller, manageable tasks. For example, if you want to manage stress better, set a milestone to practice mindfulness for five minutes each day.
- **Visualize success:** Take time to imagine yourself achieving these goals. How does it feel? What changes in your interactions? Visualization can be a powerful motivator, turning abstract goals into tangible aspirations.

Identifying Areas for Improvement

Self-reflection and feedback from trusted sources can shed light on your strengths and areas for growth. It's not about dwelling on short-comings but recognizing opportunities to enhance your emotional skills.

- **Self-reflection:** Take time to check in with yourself regularly. After social interactions or emotional experiences, ask questions like, "What went well? What could I have handled differently?"
- **Seek feedback:** Have conversations with friends, family, or mentors. Ask them where they've seen you excel and

where you might improve. Their perspectives can offer valuable insights into your emotional habits and patterns.

Resources for Learning

The journey of personal growth is enriched by the wisdom and experiences shared by others. Books, websites, and courses can be your companions, offering new perspectives and deepening your understanding of emotional intelligence.

- **Books:** Explore titles like "Emotional Intelligence 2.0" by Travis Bradberry and Jean Greaves, which provide practical strategies for boosting your EQ.
- **Websites:** Platforms like Psychology Today offer articles covering various topics related to emotional intelligence and mental health.
- **Courses:** Online platforms such as Coursera and Udemy provide courses on emotional intelligence, many taught by leading experts in the field. These courses can help you deepen your understanding and practice new skills.

Staying Motivated

The journey of personal growth isn't always straightforward; it twists and turns, sometimes looping back on itself. To stay motivated, you need patience, persistence, and a gentle acknowledgment of your efforts.

- **Celebrate small wins:** Recognize every step forward, no matter how small. Did you finish your daily mindfulness practice? Give yourself a mental high-five.

- **Growth mindset:** View challenges as chances to learn, not roadblocks. A setback in managing stress is an opportunity to try new strategies, not a reason to give up.
- **Community support:** Surround yourself with people who are also committed to personal growth. Sharing experiences, challenges, and successes can keep you inspired.
- **Self-compassion:** Be kind to yourself when progress feels slow. Remember, growth isn't always linear, and every experience, good or bad, helps you develop.

As you continue with your journey toward emotional intelligence, remember that each step, choice, and reflection adds to the masterpiece of your personal growth. Your path is unique, filled with opportunities to learn, grow, and shine.

Celebrating Your Emotional Intelligence Journey: Reflecting on How Far You've Come

In the pursuit of personal growth, it's common to overlook the progress you've made. You're so focused on where you're headed that you forget to acknowledge how far you've already come. This phase of your journey is about taking a moment to pause, look back, and give yourself a well-deserved pat on the back.

Recognizing Growth

Every time you chose to respond instead of react, paused to consider someone else's perspective, or managed stress more effectively, you were growing. Emotional intelligence growth can be subtle, like the gradual bloom of a flower. It's important to acknowledge these changes, no matter how small they may seem. They are signs of your evolving emotional landscape. Think of them as milestones, marking the path you've taken on your journey toward deeper self-understanding and empathy.

Reflective Celebration

A meaningful way to recognize your progress is through reflective celebration. Consider writing a letter to your future self, outlining the progress you've made and the challenges you've conquered. Imagine opening this letter a year from now—what would you want it to convey? This practice not only acknowledges your growth but also sets intentions for ongoing development. It serves as a reminder that the journey of emotional intelligence is continuous and that every step forward deserves celebration.

Sharing Your Journey

Opening up about your emotional intelligence journey can deepen connections and offer support, both for you and for others. When you share your experiences, you invite others into your world, showing them the potential rewards of their own efforts in emotional growth.

This sharing creates a sense of community and mutual encouragement. It demonstrates that while our experiences may differ, the emotions and challenges we face often resonate on a universal level. Whether through conversations with loved ones or on social media, letting others in on your journey can amplify the joy of your accomplishments and offer comfort during setbacks.

Continued Growth

Embracing the idea that emotional intelligence is a lifelong journey sets the stage for a future filled with personal discovery and connections. It means staying curious, open to new experiences, and willing to learn from both the highs and lows. This mindset ensures that the journey remains dynamic, offering fresh insights and opportunities for growth. It's about eagerly anticipating the next chapter, armed with the knowledge that every challenge presents a chance to expand your emotional understanding.

As you reflect on your emotional intelligence journey, you can see personal achievements, moments of connection, and valuable lessons learned. These experiences serve as milestones on your path so far and guide you toward the future. They remind you that in the realm of emotions, every step taken brings you closer to understanding, resilience, and deeper connections with yourself and others. Carry the wisdom of the past with you as you face the future with an open and wise heart.

Your final challenge awaits at the end of this book: The 14-Day Journaling Challenge.

TELL US WHAT YOU REALLY THINK ON AMAZON!

Think of your pals who might dig this book – there could be a bunch. Your thoughts matter because they help other teens dealing with similar stuff understand why emotional intelligence is key. Take a quick minute to jot down your review on Amazon. You're the best, thank you.

CONCLUSION
NEW HORIZONS: CONTINUING THE JOURNEY BEYOND

"The journey of a thousand miles begins with a single step." — Lao Tzu

AS WE WRAP up this book, I'm thinking about all the stories we've shared, both loud and quiet, that have been a part of your journey. We've been through a lot, diving into how to handle emotions and tackle the challenges of growing up in today's tech-driven world. But remember, the real magic isn't just in these pages – it's in you. You've shown bravery in facing your feelings and dealing with the ups and downs of being a teen with strength and determination.

You've covered the basics of emotional intelligence: knowing yourself, controlling your actions, understanding others, and handling relationships. These aren't just fancy ideas; they're the tools that help you feel sure of yourself, navigate the rollercoaster of teen feelings, and form genuine connections in a world that can sometimes seem shallow.

Don't forget the hands-on tips I've given you: the breathing exercises for when things get crazy, the journaling prompts to help you think things through, and the mindfulness tricks to keep you grounded. These are like your trusty compass and map, leading you toward inner calm and strength.

The stories and activities focused on understanding others, listening well, and talking effectively have all been about showing you how to form real connections. When screens take over, these abilities are what help you connect genuinely with others in a world that sometimes feels disconnected.

Nailing emotional intelligence in the digital world isn't easy. But with the tips on handling social media stress, cyberbullying, and staying healthy online, I'm confident you're more ready to tackle these hurdles. The online world keeps changing, but so do you – you're adaptable and growing all the time.

Remember, learning about yourself and growing never stops. The challenges and experiments at the end of this book are just the start – they're nudging you to keep digging into what matters to you, what you're good at, and where you can do better. It's through this exploration that you really get to know yourself.

Now, as you get ready to use what you've learned in your everyday life, I want to push you to handle every challenge with strength, understand others with care, and embrace the twists and turns of personal growth with open arms. Your journey is yours alone, full of possibilities. Believe in your power to use emotional intelligence, not just for yourself, but for the happiness and connection it brings to your life.

I'm eager to hear about your own experiences – the ups, the downs, and everything in between. Let's keep this conversation going beyond these pages, creating a space where we can all share and learn from each other's journeys.

As we go our separate ways, for now, I want to leave you with this idea: "Emotional intelligence isn't about controlling others, but about understanding ourselves, forming deep bonds with others, and handling our feelings with kindness and insight." Your journey is just getting started, and I have full faith in your ability to thrive in the digital world and beyond. When you reflect on your journey, take a look back at the challenges, experiments, or tasks given to you at the end of this book.

Here's to your ongoing growth and accomplishments. May you always find strength in being open, wisdom in looking back, and happiness in connecting with others.

21-DAY EQ CHALLENGE

Welcome to the 21-Day EQ Challenge! Get ready for a journey that'll change how you understand and handle your emotions. Follow these steps below, and in just three weeks, you'll see your emotional intelligence soar.

Week 1: Paying Attention and Understanding Your Feelings

DAY 1-3: CHECKING IN WITH YOURSELF

Grab something to write on, whether it's a notebook, your phone, or a computer. A few times each day, find a quiet spot, close your eyes, and take three deep breaths. Then, ask yourself, "How do I feel right now?" Write down what comes to mind. This is the start of becoming more aware of your feelings.

DAY 4-7: TRACKING YOUR EMOTIONS

Keep up with your check-ins. And now, start keeping a diary of your emotions. Write down moments in your day that stand out and the feelings you had during those times. At the end of the week, take a look back at what you've written. Do you notice any patterns or things that tend to trigger certain emotions? It's all about accepting all your feelings and watching them without judging yourself.

Week 2: Understanding Your Feelings Better

DAY 8-14: ASKING "WHY" FIVE TIMES

Keep up with your check-ins and emotion tracking. When you feel a strong emotion, ask yourself why you feel that way. Then, ask "why" four more times for each answer you come up with. This helps you dig deeper into why you're feeling a certain way and understand the different layers behind your emotions. By doing this, you'll gain insight into what's really causing your feelings.

Week 3: Connecting Your Mind and Body

DAY 15-21: BODY SCAN MEDITATION

Continue with your previous exercises and add the Body Scan Meditation to your routine. Take some time each day to practice this mindfulness exercise. Pay attention to any physical sensations you feel without judging them, and try to connect them with your emotional state. This helps you strengthen the connection between your mind and body, which is important for understanding your emotions in a more holistic way.

Well done for taking on this 21-Day EQ Challenge! By joining in these exercises to understand your emotions, you're investing in yourself and your development. Keep going, think about what you're learning, and enjoy the process of discovering more about yourself. Get set to explore your emotional world with a clearer mind and stronger resilience!

DAILY BREATHING CHALLENGE

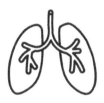

Welcome to your Daily Breathing Challenge! Each day, you'll engage in exercises designed to reset your stress levels and promote emotional regulation through deep and rhythmic breathing techniques. Let's embark on this journey toward a calmer, more centered you.

DAY 1: INTRODUCTION TO DEEP BREATHING

- **Objective:** Learn deep breathing to help reduce stress.
- **Activity: (1) Find Your Quiet Spot:** Pick a peaceful place where you won't be disturbed. **(2) Get Comfortable:** Sit or lie down in a comfy position, keeping your back straight if you're sitting. **(3) Position Your Hands:** Place one hand on your belly and the other on your chest. **(4) Breathe Deeply:** Follow these steps for 5 minutes: Inhale slowly, hold your breath, then exhale slowly.

- **Reflection:** After you finish, write down how your stress level or mood has changed.

DAY 2: MASTERING DEEP BREATHING

- **Objective:** Improve your deep breathing skills and extend your practice time.
- **Activity:** Repeat the deep breathing exercise from Day 1, but gradually increase your session to 10 minutes.
- **Challenge:** Focus on the rise and fall of your belly, trying to minimize the movement of your chest as much as possible.

DAY 3: INTRODUCTION TO RHYTHMIC BREATHING

- **Objective:** Learn and practice the 4-7-8 rhythmic breathing technique to better manage your emotions.
- **Activity:** Practice the 4-7-8 breathing technique for 4 cycles: (1) Inhale through your nose for 4 seconds. (2) Hold your breath for 7 seconds. (3) Exhale through your mouth for 8 seconds.
- **Reflection:** Note any changes in your emotional state or anxiety levels before and after the exercise.

DAY 4: COMBINING TECHNIQUES

- **Objective:** Blend deep breathing and rhythmic breathing in a single session.
- **Activity:** Start with 5 minutes of deep breathing. Follow this with 4 cycles of the 4-7-8 rhythmic breathing technique (Inhale for 4 seconds, hold for 7 seconds, exhale for 8 seconds).

- **Note:** Pay attention to how it feels to switch between the two techniques and observe how your body and mind respond.

DAY 5: DEEP BREATHING IN DIFFERENT SETTINGS

- **Objective:** Practice deep breathing in a new environment or situation.
- **Activity:** Choose a different spot or a mildly stressful situation (e.g., before starting work) and practice deep breathing for 5 minutes.
- **Reflection:** Note any differences in your experience or the effectiveness of the technique in this new setting.

DAY 6: RHYTHMIC BREATHING CHALLENGE

- **Objective:** Integrate rhythmic breathing into your daily activities.
- **Activity:** Practice the 4-7-8 technique before a specific event (e.g., meeting, presentation) or whenever you feel anxious throughout the day.
- **Note:** Observe how this technique affects your readiness and calmness in different scenarios.

DAY 7: REFLECTION AND ROUTINE

- **Objective:** Reflect on your week of breathing exercises and plan how to incorporate these techniques into your daily routine.
- **Activity:** Write down your thoughts on the past week's practice, any benefits you've noticed, and how you plan to

continue incorporating these breathing techniques into your life.

- **Challenge:** Set a goal for the next week to practice deep or rhythmic breathing at least once a day, choosing the technique that you found most beneficial.

Congratulations on completing your Daily Breathing Challenge! Remember, these techniques are tools you can use anytime, anywhere. Keep practicing, and enjoy the calm and focus they bring to your life.

EMPATHY ACTIVATION CHALLENGE

Welcome to the Empathy Activation Challenge, where the goal is to consciously engage in acts of empathy over the course of a week, reinforcing the invisible thread of connection through understanding, sharing, and kindness.

Daily Tasks:

DAY 1: REFLECTION AND CONNECTION

Think about a time when someone showed you empathy. How did it make you feel? Share this experience with a friend or family member and talk about how empathy affects relationships.

DAY 2: PERSPECTIVE-TAKING

Pick a friend or family member and try to see things from their point of view for a whole day. At the end of the day, talk to them about what you learned and ask if you got their feelings and thoughts right.

DAY 3: EMPATHETIC LISTENING

Have at least one conversation where you focus only on listening to understand, not to reply. Use active listening skills like nodding, making eye contact, and repeating back what the speaker says in your own words.

DAY 4: EMOTION LABELING EXERCISE

Talk with a friend who's going through a tough time. Work together to name the emotions they're feeling. Discuss how naming these emotions might help them manage their feelings better.

DAY 5: EMPATHY JOURNAL

Think about your interactions today. Write down times when you felt a strong connection with someone through empathy. Note how these moments affected both you and the other person.

DAY 6: ACTIVE LISTENING IN DIGITAL CONVERSATIONS

Use active listening skills in your online chats. Take a moment to really understand messages before you reply, use kind words to show empathy, and clarify or summarize to make sure you understand correctly.

DAY 7: RANDOM ACTS OF KINDNESS

Do at least three random acts of kindness. It could be as easy as giving someone a compliment, helping out a family member without them asking, or leaving a nice note for a stranger to find.

Reflection: As you wrap up the week, take a moment to think about how this challenge affected your understanding and use of empathy. Here are some questions to consider:

- How did actively practicing empathy change the way you interacted with friends and family?

- Did you observe any changes in your relationships or how people reacted to you?
- What insights did you gain about yourself and your capacity to empathize with others?

Well done on finishing the Empathy Activation Challenge! This challenge is all about making empathy a more deliberate and conscious part of your everyday interactions. By doing so, you're not only strengthening your connections with others but also contributing to a more understanding and caring community. Keep up the great work!

MINDFUL POSTING CHALLENGE

Welcome to The Mindful Posting Challenge! The goal is to cultivate awareness and responsibility in digital communication for one week.

<u>Daily Tasks:</u>

1. REFLECT BEFORE YOU SHARE

Every day, before you post anything, take a whole minute to think. Ask yourself:

- How would I feel if someone posted this about me?
- Could it be misunderstood or upset someone?
- Am I okay with everyone, including future employers or my family, seeing this?
- Does this post contribute positively to the conversation, and is it kind?

2. PRIVACY CHECK

Review your privacy settings on one social media platform each day to make sure you're aware of who can see your posts. Adjust them if needed.

3. POSITIVE INTERACTIONS ONLY

Commit to leaving only positive, supportive, or helpful comments on others' posts.

4. REPORT AND SUPPORTIVE

If you come across any cyberbullying, report it. Then, reach out to the person being bullied with a supportive message or offer to chat.

5. AUTHENTIC CONNECTIONS

Share something real about your day or interests without giving away too much personal info. It could be a thought, a hobby, a non-personal photo, or an experience.

6. DIGITAL FOOTPRINT REVIEW

Search your name on a search engine and check what's out there about you online. If you find something you'd rather keep private, take steps to remove it.

7. OFFLINE REFLECTION

Spend at least 30 minutes at the end of your day away from screens. Think about your online interactions and how they fit with your real-life values and who you are.

End-of-Week Reflection:

- Did this challenge change the way you think about posting and interacting online?
- Have your feelings about digital permanence and privacy evolved?
- Will you change your digital habits moving forward?

Remember, this challenge isn't about being perfect; it's about being more aware of your online presence and actions. Good luck!

GROWTH MINDSET EXPERIMENT

Welcome to the Growth Mindset Experiment! This experiment is to actively engage with failures, setbacks, or challenges for one week, transforming them into opportunities for growth and learning.

<u>Daily Activities:</u>

DAY 1: BOUNCING BACK FROM FAILURE

- Think about a time when something didn't go as planned. Describe what went wrong and how it made you feel. This will be a starting point to see how things improve over the week.

DAY 2: SEEING THINGS DIFFERENTLY

- Look back at what you wrote on **Day 1**. Now, tell the story again, but this time, think about what you can learn from it.

How does thinking this way make you feel about the setback?

DAY 3: LEARNING FROM MISTAKES

- Think about a small mistake you made today or recently. Figure out what you can learn from it. Then, make a small change based on this lesson. Write down what you did and how it turned out.

DAY 4: TAKING ON A CHALLENGE

- Pick something you've been avoiding because you're scared you might mess up. Spend at least 30 minutes giving it a shot. Jot down how you're feeling, what problems you run into, and any progress you make.

DAY 5: GETTING HELPFUL HINTS

- Find someone—either a friend, family member, or teacher— to give you feedback on something you're trying to get better at. Focus on taking in their feedback well, and figure out one thing you can do based on what they said.

DAY 6: LENDING A HAND

- Send a message to someone who's going through a tough time or who's had a setback lately. Offer them your support and share a story from your own life where you faced a challenge and came out stronger. Hopefully, it'll give them a boost.

DAY 7: LOOKING BACK AND MOVING FORWARD

- Take some time to think about the past week. What did you figure out about yourself and how you handle tough stuff? Write down a big goal you have for the future and map out the first few steps you need to take, thinking with your new growth mindset.

Sharing and Reflection:

At the end of the week, it's cool to talk about what you went through and what you figured out. Here are some things you could chat about:

- How did doing those daily activities make you think differently about failing and dealing with tough stuff?
- What was the hardest thing about doing this experiment, and why was it tough for you?
- How are you going to use what you learned this week when you face tough stuff in the future?

This experiment is all about making the idea of having a growth mindset real for you. By actually doing stuff and thinking about what happens, you start to see that failing isn't the end of the world—it's just part of getting where you want to go. Nice job giving it a go!

DIGITAL DETOX CHALLENGE

Welcome to the Digital Detox Challenge! For the next week, you'll dial back on the screen time, get back to some real-world living, and find a better balance with your digital life. Here's what's coming up:

DAY 1: GETTING IN THE KNOW & SETTING UP

- Start by keeping track of how much time you spend glued to your screens. Then, figure out what you hope to get out of this detox—whether it's more time for fun stuff, better sleep, or just being more focused. Lastly, let your friends and family know about your plans so they can give you a hand.

DAY 2: OFF THE GRID & THINKING IT OVER

- Time to quiet those buzzing notifications and ditch the apps that eat up too much of your day. Take a moment to think about how it feels to disconnect a bit and jot down your thoughts.

DAY 3: FINDING FUN STUFF AGAIN

- Block out at least two hours to dive into a hobby or something fun without any screens butting in. Afterward, write down how it felt and how it compared to your usual screen-heavy routine.

DAY 4: NATURE TIME

- Take a stroll, hit the trails, or just chill outside for at least an hour. And here's the twist—leave your phone at home or switch it to do-not-disturb mode.

DAY 5: GET LOST IN A GOOD BOOK

- Spend at least an hour diving into a book or magazine just for fun. Afterward, chat about what you're reading with a friend or family member, face to face.

DAY 6: GET MOVING

- Get your body moving with some yoga, dancing, or whatever physical activity you're into, and keep it screen-free. Then, think about how your body feels during and after the activity.

DAY 7: REFLECT & RECONNECT

- Wrap up the week with some quality face-to-face time with friends or family. And while you're at it, think about what you've learned about your digital habits over the past week.

Keep It Going: Finding that Sweet Spot

- Set up some specific times when you're allowed to use your devices.
- Keep up with your hobbies, reading, and staying active on the regular.
- Take a moment each week to think about how much time you're spending online and make tweaks as needed to keep things in check.

Just a reminder: This challenge isn't about ditching technology completely. It's all about finding a better balance with it. Have fun with your digital detox adventure, and best of luck!

DIGITAL KINDNESS EXPERIMENT

Welcome to The Digital Kindness Experiment! This experiment is here to help you use what you've learned about making and keeping friends online, setting healthy boundaries, avoiding toxic relationships, and building a positive digital community. For the next seven days, you'll take on different challenges to boost your online skills, focusing on empathy, kindness, and being real.

DAY 1: RECIPROCITY CHECK

- Start a conversation with at least two online friends by commenting on their posts or sending them messages. Give genuine compliments or show interest in what they posted. See if and how they respond. Think about how their response makes you feel and if it changes how you see the friendship.

Let's continue...

DAY 2: BOUNDARY SETTING

- Pick a boundary that's important to you in one of your online friendships or on social media. Clearly communicate this boundary to your friend(s) or adjust your privacy settings as needed. Note any challenges you face in sticking to this boundary and how it affects your relationship.

DAY 3: DETOX DAY

- Take a break from social media for a whole day. Spend time doing things you enjoy offline. Pay attention to how you feel throughout the day. Do you feel relieved, anxious, disconnected, or something else? Write a short reflection about your experience.

DAY 4: POSITIVE IMPACT CHALLENGE

- Pick three people from your online circle and do something kind for each of them. This could be leaving a supportive comment, sharing a resource they might like, or just sending a message to check-in. Notice how they react and how these acts of kindness make you feel.

DAY 5: TOXIC RELATIONSHIP REFLECTION

- Think about your online friendships and identify any that might be toxic. Use the criteria from the chapter (constant negativity, manipulation, disrespect for boundaries) to help you. Plan how to either address these issues with the person or distance yourself from the relationship.

You are almost there!

DAY 6: CREATE AND SHARE

- Make a post or digital creation that shows something true about yourself or something you're passionate about. This could be a hobby, a belief, a personal achievement, or a challenge you're facing. Share it with your online community. Pay attention to and document the responses you get.

DAY 7: REFLECTION

- At the end of the week, write about your experience. Focus on what you learned about yourself, your online friendships, and how your digital behavior affects things. Think about these questions:

1. How did practicing kindness and empathy online change your digital interactions and friendships?
2. Were there any surprises or challenges in setting and enforcing boundaries?
3. How did the detox day change your view on social media use?
4. What did you learn about being authentic and vulnerable online through creating and sharing a personal post?

I encourage you to share your reflections and insights in a dedicated online space, creating a community of learning and support. This could be a class blog, a social media group, or a video-sharing platform.

21-DAY EMOTIONAL WELLNESS JOURNEY CHALLENGE

Welcome to the 21-Day Emotional Wellness Journey Challenge! This challenge will take you on a three-week journey to explore and integrate practices that promote emotional well-being, mindfulness, healthy sleep patterns, balanced nutrition, and creative expression.

<u>Weekly Focus and Daily Tasks:</u>

WEEK 1: SELF-CARE AND MINDFULNESS

DAY 1: Write down your current self-care habits. Pick one new self-care activity to add to your daily routine.

DAY 2: Start a mindfulness practice. Spend 5 minutes doing mindful breathing.

DAY 3: Do a physical activity you enjoy. Notice how it affects your mood afterward.

DAY 4: Practice gratitude. Write down three things you're grateful for today.

DAY 5: Take a break from screens for an evening. Reflect on how it affects your mood.

DAY 6: Try a new relaxing activity, like taking a warm bath or reading a book for fun.

DAY 7: Reflect on your week of self-care. What did you enjoy the most? How can you do more of it?

WEEK 2: SLEEP AND NUTRITION

DAY 8: Check your sleep environment and make one change to help you sleep better (like using blackout curtains).

DAY 9: Set a regular bedtime and wake-up time to get your sleep schedule on track.

DAY 10: Add a healthy, nutrient-rich food to your diet. Notice how it affects your mood and energy levels.

DAY 11: Eat one meal mindfully, focusing completely on the experience without distractions.

DAY 12: Create a relaxing bedtime routine that doesn't involve screens. Notice if your sleep improves.

DAY 13: Think about your food choices. Identify one change to support your emotional well-being.

DAY 14: Write about how your sleep and nutrition habits affect your mood. Plan how to keep up the good habits.

WEEK 3: CREATIVE EXPRESSION

DAY 15: Pick a creative activity (like writing, drawing, or playing music) and spend 30 minutes on it.

DAY 16: Share something you created with a friend or family member. Reflect on how sharing made you feel.

DAY 17: Try a new creative activity you've never done before. Notice how it affects your emotions.

DAY 18: Attend an arts event at school or in your community. Pay attention to how it influences your mood and thoughts.

DAY 19: Use your favorite creative activity to express your feelings today.

DAY 20: Work on a creative project with a friend or group. Notice how collaborating affects your mood.

DAY 21: Look back on the last three weeks. Identify which activities helped you the most. Plan how to keep these practices in your daily life.

Sharing and Reflection:

After finishing the challenge, it's a great idea to talk about your experiences and thoughts with others. You can share on social media or have a chat with friends or family.

Here are some questions to consider:

- What did you learn about yourself during this challenge?
- Which activities had the biggest positive effect on how you felt?
- How do you plan to keep doing these things in your life?

This 21-day journey is meant to give you lots of ways to take care of your emotional health. It encourages you to try out different things and see what works best for you. Keep it up—you're doing great!

14-DAY JOURNALING CHALLENGE

Welcome to your 14-Day Journaling Challenge! For the next two weeks, you'll be taking part in different journaling activities. These exercises are meant to help you explore and understand your emotions, what sets them off, any recurring themes, and how well you understand and handle your feelings overall. Let's dive in and discover more about your emotional intelligence together!

Daily Tasks and Prompts:

WEEK 1: EXPLORATION AND AWARENESS

DAY 1: STREAM OF CONSCIOUSNESS JOURNALING

- Set aside 10 minutes to write whatever comes to mind. Let your thoughts and feelings flow freely onto the page without editing or censoring.

You got this!

DAY 2: EMOTION-FOCUSED ENTRY

- Pick one emotion that you felt strongly today. Describe what triggered this emotion, how it showed up in your thoughts and actions, and how you dealt with it.

DAY 3: GRATITUDE JOURNALING

- Write about three things you're grateful for and why. Try to think about different parts of your life, big or small, and appreciate them.

DAY 4: THE PUZZLE OF EMOTIONS

- Think about a recent situation where your emotions caught you off guard. Write about what you felt, why you think you felt that way, and what you learned from the experience.

DAY 5: LETTER TO MYSELF

- Compose a letter to yourself showing understanding and kindness about a recent challenge you faced. Highlight your strengths and how they can help you overcome future obstacles.

DAY 6: FUTURE SELF VISUALIZATION

- Imagine where you want to be emotionally a year from now. Describe this future version of yourself, focusing on your emotional growth and how you achieved it.

Almost halfway there!

Don't give up!

DAY 7: REFLECTION ON WEEK 1

- Look back on what you've written this week. Write about any patterns or insights you've discovered about your emotional reactions and triggers.

WEEK 2: REGULATION AND GROWTH

DAY 8: PROBLEM-SOLVING ENTRY

- Think about a challenge you're dealing with right now. Write down potential solutions and explore the emotions each solution brings up for you.

DAY 9: THE ROLE OF FEAR

- Reflect on something that scares you and delve into the emotions behind that fear. How can you deal with these feelings in a positive way?

DAY 10: INSPIRATIONAL FIGURE ENTRY

- Pick someone you admire for their emotional intelligence— Journal about the qualities they have and how you can develop those qualities in yourself.

DAY 11: THE EMOTIONAL IMPACT OF SELF-CARE

- Think about your self-care routines and how they affect your emotions. Are there any new practices you want to try out?

Look! You're already 11 days in.

DAY 12: EMOTIONAL GOAL SETTING

- Considering what you've discovered about yourself, set three emotional goals for the next month. Plan out the steps you'll take to accomplish each one.

DAY 13: LETTER FROM MY FUTURE SELF

- Write a letter as if it's from your future self, congratulating you on the emotional progress you've made. What advice would your future self offer you?

DAY 14: CELEBRATION OF GROWTH

- Reflect on the past two weeks. Write about how this challenge has influenced your awareness and handling of your emotions. Celebrate your dedication to emotional development.

Sharing and Reflection:

You're encouraged to share any insights or breakthroughs you've had during the challenge with a friend, family member, or mentor. Whether you choose to talk about it or share selected journal entries, discussing your journey can deepen your understanding and strengthen your connections with others who are on a similar path.

What an incredible journey you've embarked on! I'm eagerly anticipating where your emotional intelligence will take you next.

TEENS TACKLING TODAY BOOK COLLECTION

The Power of Self-Love for Teen Girls: Learn How to Embrace Your Uniqueness to Create a Life Filled with Confidence, Self-Acceptance, and Long-Lasting, Genuine Relationships

Mastering Emotional Intelligence for Teens: Thrive in the Digital Age with a Positive Mindset, Build Resilience, Embrace Growth, and Navigate Social Media

REFERENCES

Aacap. (n.d.). *Teen brain: behavior, problem solving, and decision making.* https://www.aacap.org/AACAP/Families_and_Youth/Fact s_for_Families/FFF-Guide/The-Teen-Brain-Behavior-Problem-Solv ing-and-Decision-Making-095.aspx

Active listening with pre-teens and teenagers. (2024, March 6). Raising Children Network. https://raisingchildren.net.au/pre-teens/ communicating-relationships/communicating/active-listening

"A single act of kindness throws out roots in all directions, and the roots spring up and make new trees." —Amelia Earhart. (n.d.). The Foundation for a Better Life. https://www.passiton.com/inspira tional-quotes/7491-a-single-act-of-kindness-throws-out-roots-in

A quote by Deborah Day. (n.d.). https://www.goodreads.com/quotes/ 557406-nourishing-yourself-in-a-way-that-helps-you-blossom-in

A quote by Lee Iacocca. (n.d.). https://www.goodreads.com/quotes/ 328040-the-discipline-of-writing-something-down-is-the-first-step

A quote by Lao Tzu. (n.d.). https://www.goodreads.com/quotes/21535-the-journey-of-a-thousand-miles-begins-with-a-single

A quote by Mohsin Hamid. (n.d.). https://www.goodreads.com/quotes/9076745-empathy-is-about-finding-echoes-of-another-person-in-yourself

A quote by Ralph Waldo Emerson. (n.d.). https://www.goodreads.com/quotes/27820-the-only-way-to-have-a-friend-is-to-be

A quote by William James. (n.d.). https://www.goodreads.com/quotes/10301-the-greatest-discovery-of-any-generation-is-that-a-human

A quote by Vironika Tugaleva. (n.d.). https://www.goodreads.com/quotes/7707485-emotions-are-not-problems-to-be-solved-they-are-signals

A quote from Harry Potter and the Deathly Hallows. (n.d.). https://www.goodreads.com/quotes/723814-words-are-in-my-not-so-humble-opinion-our-most-inexhaustible-source

A quote from Running with the Mind of Meditation. (n.d.). https://www.goodreads.com/quotes/988868-the-body-benefits-from-movement-and-the-mind-benefits-from

Austin, A. (2023, June 9). *5 Strategies for Teaching Empathy to Teens.* https://www.connectionsacademy.com/support/resources/article/teaching-empathy-to-teens/

Brukner, L. (2021, May 24). *Emotional regulation activities for tweens and teens.* Edutopia. https://www.edutopia.org/article/emotional-regulation-activities-tweens-and-teens/

Chen, L. Y. (2023). Influence of music on the hearing and mental health of adolescents and countermeasures. *Frontiers in Neuroscience, 17.* https://doi.org/10.3389/fnins.2023.1236638

Connor-Savarda, B. (2023, April 1). *The power of emotional intelligence in the face of peer pressure*. EI Magazine. https://www.ei-magazine.com/post/the-power-of-emotional-intelligence-in-the-face-of-peer-pressure

Cortisol (Blood) - Health Encyclopedia - University of Rochester Medical Center. (n.d.). https://www.urmc.rochester.edu/encyclopedia/content.aspx?contenttypeid=167&contentid=cortisol_serum

Department of Health & Human Services. (n.d.). *Teenagers and communication*. Better Health Channel. https://www.betterhealth.vic.gov.au/health/healthyliving/teenagers-and-communication

DigCIT landing Page | Common Sense Education. (n.d.). Common Sense Education. https://www.commonsense.org/education/digital-citizenship

Ehmke, R., Steiner-Adair, C., EdD, & Wick, D., EdD. (2023, August 10). *How using social media affects teenagers*. Child Mind Institute. https://childmind.org/article/how-using-social-media-affects-teenagers/

Espino, E., Guarini, A., & Del Rey, R. (2023). Effective coping with cyberbullying in boys and girls: the mediating role of self-awareness, responsible decision-making, and social support. *Current Psychology*, 42(36), 32134–32146. https://doi.org/10.1007/s12144-022-04213-5

Frederick, E. (2021, August 19). *18 awesome technology quotes to Inspire & Motivate*. Criteria for Success. https://criteriaforsuccess.com/18-awesome-technology-quotes-to-inspire-motivate/

Internet Matters Ltd. (2023, October 30). *Helping young people manage their online identity - Internet Matters*. Internet Matters. https://www.internetmatters.org/resources/helping-young-people-manage-their-online-identity/

Janelle. (2022, February 21). *12 stories of failure before success that will inspire you.* Ellanyze. https://ellanyze.com/12-stories-of-failure-before-success-that-will-inspire-you/

Journaling for mental health. (n.d.). Stanford Medicine Children's Health. https://www.stanfordchildrens.org/en/topic/default?id=journaling-for-mental-health-1-4552

Lparsons. (2022, November 9). *8 Time Management Tips for Students - Harvard Summer School.* Harvard Summer School. https://summer.harvard.edu/blog/8-time-management-tips-for-students/

Mandriota, M. (2022, June 30). *7 mindfulness exercises for teens and tips to get started.* Psych Central. https://psychcentral.com/health/the-benefits-of-mindfulness-meditation-for-teens

Mathew, H. S. (2023, May 25). *10 netiquette rules your teen must observe to be respectful and keep safe on the internet.* Shri Harini Media Ltd. https://www.parentcircle.com/internet-etiquette-rules-for-teens/article

More sleep could improve many U.S. teenagers' mental health. (n.d.). PRB. https://www.prb.org/resources/more-sleep-could-improve-many-u-s-teenagers-mental-health/

MSc, O. G. (2023, November 9). *Fight, flight, freeze, or fawn: How we respond to threats.* Simply Psychology. https://www.simplypsychology.org/fight-flight-freeze-fawn.html

Nixon, C. L. (2014). Current perspectives: the impact of cyberbullying on adolescent health. *Adolescent Health, Medicine and Therapeutics, 143.* https://doi.org/10.2147/ahmt.s36456

O'Neil, A., Quirk, S. E., Housden, S., Brennan, S. L., Williams, L. J., Pasco, J. A., Berk, M., & Jacka, F. N. (2014). Relationship between Diet and Mental Health in Children and Adolescents: A Systematic review. *American Journal of Public Health*, 104(10), e31–e42. https://doi.org/10.2105/ajph.2014.302110

Pathway2success. (2023, October 27). 30 *Gratitude Activities for kids and teens - The Pathway 2 Success*. The Pathway 2 Success. https://www.thepathway2success.com/30-gratitude-activities-for-kids-and-teens/

Resilience for teens: 10 tips to build skills on bouncing back from rough times. (2020, June 1). *https://www.apa.org*. https://www.apa.org/topics/resilience/bounce-teens

Sesso, G., Brancati, G. E., Fantozzi, P., Inguaggiato, E., Milone, A., & Masi, G. (2021). Measures of empathy in children and adolescents: A systematic review of questionnaires. *World Journal of Psychiatry*, 11(10), 876–896. https://doi.org/10.5498/wjp.v11.i10.876

(7) *The role of art and creativity in teen emotional expression and coping | LinkedIn*. (2023, August 21). https://www.linkedin.com/pulse/role-art-creativity-teen-emotional-expression-coping-skitii/

Social media and youth mental health — current priorities of the U.S. Surgeon General. (n.d.). https://www.hhs.gov/surgeongeneral/priorities/youth-mental-health/social-media/index.html

Staff, N. A. (2022, October 6). How teens can practice reframing negative thoughts. *Newport Academy*. https://www.newportacademy.com/resources/mental-health/reframing-negative-thoughts/

Staff, N. A. (2023, January 5). Building resilience in children and teens. *Newport Academy*. https://www.newportacademy.com/resources/well-being/resilience-in-teens/

Staff, N. A. (2024, January 17). How to help teens unplug. *Newport Academy*. https://www.newportacademy.com/resources/restoring-families/digital-detox/

Students do better in school when they can understand, manage emotions. (2019, December 12). *https://www.apa.org*. https://www.apa.org/news/press/releases/2019/12/students-manage-emotions

Teens and social media use: What's the impact? (2024, January 18). Mayo Clinic. https://www.mayoclinic.org/healthy-lifestyle/tween-and-teen-health/in-depth/teens-and-social-media-use/art-20474437

What are some ways to find a mentor who can help with emotional intelligence and self-awareness? (n.d.). https://www.linkedin.com/advice/1/what-some-ways-find-mentor-who-can-help-emotional-intelligence-hxxqe

Weinstein, T. (2024, January 24). How to help teens build emotional intelligence. *Newport Academy*. https://www.newportacademy.com/resources/empowering-teens/teen-emotional-intelligence/

Whitworth, J. (2023, March 23). Six mental health benefits of exercise in Teens - Trails Carolina. *Trails Carolina*. https://trailscarolina.com/blog/six-mental-health-benefits-exercise-teens/

Wright, K. W., & Wright, K. W. (2023, November 2). *8 Benefits of journaling for mental health*. Day One | Your Journal for Life. https://dayoneapp.com/blog/benefits-of-journaling-for-mental-health/

Made in the USA
Monee, IL
21 December 2024